These Rebellious Powers

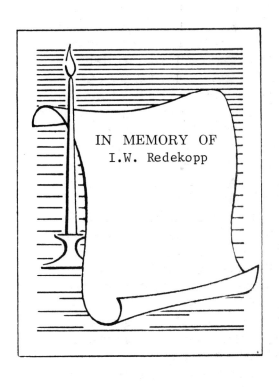

IN MEMORY OF
I.W. Redekopp

THESE
REBELLIOUS
POWERS

by *Albert H. van den Heuvel*

FRIENDSHIP PRESS
new york

All Bible quotations in this book, unless otherwise noted, are from the Revised Standard Version, copyright, 1946 and 1952, by the Division of Christian Education of the National Council of the Churches of Christ in the United States of America, and *The New English Bible, New Testament,* copyright, The Delegates of the Oxford University Press and The Syndics of the Cambridge University Press, 1961, reprinted by permission.

These Rebellious Powers is dedicated to
Erick and Sarah Suzanne,
whom, of all the children in the youth department family,
I had most in mind while writing it

Contents

Contents

ACKNOWLEDGMENT

This little book would not have been written if Dr. Hendrikus Berkhof had not published his *Christ and the Powers* several years ago. The second chapter is very little more—and probably much less—than a popularization of his main thesis.

Valerie Tong has helped with the organization and language of this book. If what follows is at all readable, she deserves the credit.

CHAPTER ONE

Models for Life

This is a funny book.

It is supposed to be a book on mission written for people who are just beginning that great adventure called adult life. Yet no one knows exactly when this adventure starts. Sociologists and psychologists fight quite a battle about that. And so do you, probably; adolescence and adulthood fight each other from early puberty to middle age.

This book should take into account the whole younger generation in the world. That is not a small undertaking—in fact it is impossible here to deal with all the 700 million young people in the world. Furthermore, the author is no expert. I certainly have no answers to the questions with which a younger generation is faced: I hardly have the answers to my own questions. I have an idea in which direction we should walk together, but I can give little specific guidance.

Older people tell us that the younger ones in our society are greatly confused about the questions a complex modern world is asking. They are right; but they are wrong in thinking that only the younger ones are confused. The adult generation in our age is certainly as confused as the younger one. The world that preceding generations built, in which we are now invited to take part, is divided; nation is fighting against nation. The economic situation in our world is grossly unbalanced; we and a few others are rich, and two thirds of the world is hungry. There are millions of refugees. Hate, misunderstanding, war, and crime exist all around us.

At the same time, through technology and science, we are discovering a world so exciting that we would not live in any other age. The possibilities for improving our planet and our society have never been greater. The task is to establish a productive relationship between the tensions of confusion and clarity existing today for both older and younger generations.

LET'S TALK

The best chance we have for success as generations and as nations is to come to grips with ourselves and with the world in a good, serious talk. All our cards should be thrown on the table. We should not try to answer questions that nobody asks; we should not try to dodge problems with which we are faced; and we should certainly not try to dodge questions that others in the world are asking us. So let's talk. Let us talk freely about our problems, and let us discuss freely the problems other people bring to our attention. Let us talk as responsible and responsive people, who have had the privilege of going to school and having a home where we had food, a bed, and reasonably intelligent people around us to talk with.

We should, however, check our presuppositions. We know that we belong to different communities. Most of the readers of this book will be Americans; I am a Dutchman. We probably belong to different churches, and we have little in common. Little, however, is not nothing.

We have in common the knowledge that life is tough.
The questions before us are real ones. We know that other
people expect us to be reliable. We have to choose a career.
We have to develop our talents. We have to make decisions
about race, military service, personal relationships with our
parents, friends, and dating partners pretty early in life.
Tough questions, all of them; and if we are to find answers,
they should be carefully thought out.

We also have in common the fact that we belong to a
community of faith. Some people would like to qualify that
and say: "I belong to a churchgoing family, and therefore I
was brought into that community." Others would disagree,
preferring to say that God himself knew us before we were
born and created us in the particular family in which we
grew up. Many, if not most, of us have ambivalent feelings
toward the church. "One day maybe I'll be ready for it,"
we may say. Or, "I like it, but I am not ready to commit
myself to it." Or, "I dislike it tremendously, but I don't
want to quit, because there is something in it somewhere."
Or rarely, somebody may pick up this book and say, "I want
to get out of the church, but I don't want to hurt my parents,
or I don't want to say so yet." Ambivalent feelings toward
the church and the gospel are shared by young people in all
continents.

All these reactions are valid, but they need to be exam-
ined. Commitment to the church and leaving it are pretty
serious issues and may well shape our lives. A boy who
grows up in the Christian community will have different
friends, thoughts, habits, and ideas from somebody who
joins the Communist party. That is a factual statement. Our
chosen communities carry their own little world with them,

<u>and when we choose our community we choose a whole model of life with it.</u>

Yet young people are not alone in debating their religious beliefs. Adults have the same ambivalent attitude toward the church and faith. The people who stick to the church unquestioningly are those who are too fascinated by the gospel to leave, whether they like it or not. Our conversation will start from this point: the fascination of the gospel in a world that changes extremely quickly and drastically.

So let's talk.

One more thing. Talking, conversation, dialogue, debate are not neutral words. They all produce some sort of relationship. The more deeply we talk, the more honest we are, the more difficult our conversation becomes. Really saying something always means showing just a little bit more of yourself than can be seen from the outside. It means sticking your neck out just far enough for somebody else to hit you. It means delivering yourself into the hands of your partner in the conversation. Involvement is what we want.

Lots of people babble. They use words, but they hide behind them. They are throwing up a smoke screen of words behind which they can be by themselves. We are not interested in that type of talking. We shall try to grow up and master our lives. Development is what we want.

So let's talk.

LET'S LOOK AROUND

Talking about ourselves does no good when we fail to consider our environment. We are not alone. There are a few other people on this globe, and about one third of them —in fact rather more than one third—are young. You can see them everywhere. Of course we have our schools and playgrounds and offices where we see our immediate contemporaries, and these are the people we know best. But the TV and the newspapers show us others beyond our own shores.

Our great-grandfathers did not have half the knowledge of their generation that we have about ours. They (and maybe they were lucky) knew only the people in their own towns; even the boys and girls in another part of the country were strange creatures to them. But we, today, have to live with all our generation.

The fact that we are aware of our contemporaries around the earth does not imply that we are united or even could be united. We are diverse in many ways.

First of all we are divided into two great groups. We either belong to stable societies or we belong to changing ones. The first group is getting smaller and smaller. In some areas of Asia and Africa stable societies still exist: communities where only people change and conditions remain the same. The way in which the soil is tilled, the way in which houses are built, the relations between fathers and sons, the way in which the bread is baked: all activities are repeated identically from year to year. People do not travel, and they certainly do not move to other areas. In the course of time wars are fought, the old people (and quite a few young ones) die, but the pattern of life does not change. There are usually no schools, and if they exist they teach only what the parents know. Father always knows more than son, and mother always has more experience than daughter. There is no talk about the good old days, because all days are the same. There is no hope for a better future or fear of decline. There is no generation problem, because the children gradually take over the work from the elders and all occupations have their appointed time. There is no authority clash between teachers and pupils, because authority comes with certain functions and nobody questions it. When change occurs, by accident so to speak, the new discovery or the different situation is smoothly integrated into the existing structure of society, and life continues as calmly as before.

Our counterparts in this generation are lucky, at least at first sight. For them there is no competition in the school or the community, no friction with their parents, no changing customs to keep up with, no changing slang, no changing musical stars even! Today we have to travel far to find a stable society, and those that do exist are on the verge of joining us in the race for change. In Africa there are many states in which the younger generation is just getting into the spirit of this race. Their parents are still people who were born in the stability of yesterday, when a white power was ruling their land.

The younger Africans see the change coming. Maybe a big highway is slowly eating away at the loneliness of the land; maybe a factory has been built in the middle of nowhere, and people are working there without being seen and earning more money than anyone else around. Often the church in the area will warn them, "All these new things will only bring trouble!" And so they do! The parents will get mad. "Why do you want to travel on that highway? Is life not good enough here?" "Why do you want to work in a factory? Your father and his father and his father have worked on the land, and the life was good." "Why do you want to earn more money? Money means drinking, and drinking means perdition. . . . "

We in our modern houses, amid all the pressures life brings to bear on us, can hardly imagine any longer what it is for a younger generation to be the first to pass the threshold of change. Can you still imagine what it would be to ride in a car, a train, or a bus for the first time? What it must be to see for the first time how a mechanical instrument plows the soil in one tenth of the time father, grandfather, and great-grandfather took to do it? How it must feel to be the first one in a community to be able to read or write and suddenly to have a world as large as the ocean opened up for you? What it must be to have a radio in the village for the first time and hear people speak to you, play for you, question you?

We have to think about our contemporaries in remote places, with whom we grow up as much as with those near us. When we are called to leadership and partnership in the world, and through reading, traveling, discussing, and voting enter the stage of the international world, we will see these young people as our counterparts in other parts of the world. Great issues like war and peace are related to small issues like our understanding of others' problems.

What a change when we turn our eyes to the younger generation in Europe and North America! Ours is anything but a stable society. I once heard the story in the United States of a third-grade boy who was asked to write an essay on his life. He turned in an almost blank sheet of paper. The only lines he had written were: "I was born in New York. When I was two we moved to Detroit; when I was three we moved to Denver; when I was five we moved to New Orleans; when

I was six we moved to Chicago; and now we moved here." In the big cities of Great Britain and Holland there are districts where the whole population changes in the course of five years.

People move: they move during their holidays, they move to go to work, they move to have fun, they move to go to school. All of us have experience in many communities, and we learn early to play many roles. We have one set of authorities at home, and our behavior with them is different from our behavior with the authorities in school. The authorities at home, and our behavior with them is different new set of responses. When we go to college, the school community determines our behavior to a large extent. Thus we grow into the complicated fabric of our modern society. Complexity and change are the key words to describe it.

Our context is not only geographical. The community that surrounds us is not the only influence in our education and formation. We are also living with the communities of the past: our context is historical. That should not amaze you too much. You do not have to think immediately of a country like Japan, where the cult of the ancestors determines large sections of life, so that the dead have a considerable share in the way a younger generation thinks and works. Think of Germany for instance, where everybody, old or young, has to live today with what happened during the Nazi period in the 1930's and 1940's. Newspapers report new trials for war criminals, and the atrocities of twenty years ago are recounted on TV and in the daily press. The teen-ager of Germany today was not even born when it all happened, but he lives with it. When he travels, he is questioned about it; when he talks with his parents about their youth, the shadow of that awful period of history is forever present. "Why, Dad, did your generation tolerate all that? Did you speak up for the Jews? Did you help to hide people who were on their way to the concentration camps? Did you think you were wrong or were you afraid to speak up?"

Others of our contemporaries are also affected by events in the past: those who lived through a war in recent years, for instance in Korea, or those who lived through a revolution like that of the Hungarians, the Cubans, or many of the African nations. They all live in close contact with what happened yesterday and with those who died or disappeared in those events. This background shapes their lives and hopes, and for that reason it also shapes ours. When we look around, we experience a whole new network of relationships to past, present, and future, different in all countries but always there.

CHOOSING A MODEL FOR LIFE

In this terrific pluriformity around us, all people are looking for a model on which they can base a strategy for life. Perhaps it is not fair to say that all people are *looking* for a model; they all *have* one. In the stable society the model of the younger generation is the father or mother. Young people grow up to repeat the life of the older people. They hardly think about their models, which are self-evident, given with life itself. When another tribe comes into their territory, they will give their lives for their own customs and traditions because life is guaranteed by the faithful repetition of what is known.

When the stable society breaks down, the models change. When we read about the developing countries, we are aware of the many possibilities offered to a younger generation. What became the model of life for a young African when white men came and, with their economy, their industry, their colonialism, broke down the stable society? The next thing in the African's life was that he had to choose between conflicting models: should he defend the old system; should he become like the white man (and alienate himself from his people); should he become an advocate for a real African industrial system? Conflict and tension had entered his life in a very real way, and whatever he did, the old model of life had lost its relevance. His model was no longer self-evident. The first period was the most difficult, because even when he chose, it was never a clear-cut choice between the one or the other. He defended the old system, but the means by which he fought was influenced by the white man's presence and ways; or he tried to Africanize the white man's imported ways of life while having to fight both the conservatives and those who simply wanted to imitate the newly seen realities.

Another example of ambiguous models is seen in the conflict within the younger generation in East Germany. The country was a liberal democracy until 1933. When Hitler took over, democracy was taken away. Political parties were reduced, and the only decisive political system left was the National Socialist Party of Adolf Hitler. Most of the younger generation accepted him and his philosophy as models for their lives. They dreamed of a Europe, indeed of a world, dominated by a Germany that would be a strong, pure race of Aryan type, in which there was no place for Jews or invalids: a nation worthy to lead the world. Of course the Germans would have to fight for world dominion, but they were prepared for that; and in 1941 Germany was the strongest country in Europe.

In 1945, though, their dream was shattered. Germany had become a smoking ruin under the attacks of England, America, and Russia. Six million Jews had been killed and hundreds of thousands of sick and invalid people had been put to death. A new generation in the eastern part of Germany grew up, now under the rule of the Russians and the small Communist party of the German Democratic Republic.

Again there is a dictatorship, but of a different nature from the Nazi one. The order of society has not been chosen by the people themselves, but it is much more humane than the Nazi regime. The systematic destruction of invalids and political opponents has stopped, the concentration camps have been abolished, and the people have been forced to enter an era of building up the Communist society. Thousands of people have fled to Western Germany, which has again become a liberal democracy; millions of people have stayed, either because they want to remain in their own country or because they can no longer get out.

A younger generation in East Germany now has to choose its model in a complex situation. A large group has chosen communism and works, along with the government, for the establishment of the Communist state. Among them some are happy with the current state of affairs, but a large number of young people disagree with the present regime even though they basically agree with the socialist vision. They are the critical participants who try to change the present situation from within. They do not want to go back to the prewar political system; they hope communism will one day fulfill its promises as Marx, Engels, and Lenin have described.

Another group has chosen the Western political system as its model and can hardly wait to break down the wall in Berlin. They want to tear down the iron curtain and re-establish Germany under the leadership of the West German politicians.

Thus the East German younger generation has to choose between several models. Like young people anywhere else in the world, great numbers of them do not choose at all and are content to live from day to day. They have accommodated themselves and live as securely as they can within the limits of the established society. For them there is no discussion, no commitment, no choice. Does this mean that they have no model at all? Of course not. Their model is conformity; they believe in conforming, and by their lives they witness to this belief. They have adapted themselves to the status quo and have decided to play it safe.

Let us be honest and say that the majority of young people in the world choose the model of conformity because it involves the least personal decision. How many people in the United States dare to commit themselves to the model of a fully integrated society? Are not most people content to play it safe and wait to see what will be the result of the fight for equal rights for all sections of the American people? Commitment, choice, and decision in our society always involve tension, strife, and often a great deal of loneliness. Only people who have built up a firm basic pattern of thinking and who have sorted out their responsibilities can afford to stand up and live according to their models.

We have looked briefly at two struggles to find a model, a social one in Africa and a political one in Europe. While discussing these two examples we have used words like decision, choice, commitment. The use of these words brings us to the insight that models are not only systems. They are basic attitudes. In society and all its institutions we are asked what our attitudes are—where we find our point of departure in dealing with different systems. The models we choose in social, political, and personal life apparently have an inner cohesion in the way we look at life itself. We do not only choose between democracy and communism, between an integrated society and a segregated one, between Democrats and Republicans, between colonialism and helping the struggle for freedom. We have to choose between attitudes toward all these systems, between being dogmatic and being open about them, between using them and serving them, between using them to improve our own life and using them for others, between domination and service. In other words when we look for models of life, we are looking for a basic decision about life. We are looking for a faith.

FAITH AND MODELS

Now we have to talk carefully, because here we make basic decisions. We are trying to master life. We must make choices at a number of levels: political choices, social choices, choices about how we will cope with relationships with others and ourselves. As soon as we recognize the necessity to choose, the first decision has been made: we will commit ourselves. We will look life straight in the eye and make up our minds. For these different choices we need cohesion: something or someone to serve as a starting point for our further actions and thinking. We have to make up our minds to whom or to what we shall relate our thinking. This relation we call faith; and on the basis of our faith we will have to start thinking about all the other departments of life.

Here again there are many possibilities. We can put our faith in *ourselves.* Many people do that. They have found that the only person with whom one always *has* to live is one's ego, oneself, and they choose to make the center of their lives their own egos. In America the popular writer on this theme is Ayn Rand. One of her heroes, Howard Roark, in *The Fountainhead,* says:

The first right on earth is the ego. Man's first duty is to himself. His moral obligation is to do what he wishes, provided his wish does not depend primarily on other people. This includes the whole sphere of his creative faculty, his thinking, his work.*

Many of the modern sciences of man, like psychology and psychiatry, run the danger of concentrating too much on man as the center of his own universe. These sciences, which were originally designed to restore man to his community, tend to become cheap means of satisfying our own original egotism when they are popularized. We must be aware that egotism is a faith which is a live option for each one of us.

In contrast to egotism, there is a faith called *altruism.* An altruistic person centers his attention on other people and places his concern for their well-being before everything else. He can only be happy when he is doing good for others.

A third faith is *materialism.* At the center of this faith lies the affirmation that the only real thing that exists is matter. Man forms part of it, and so do all existing objects. Our task in life is to relate to matter, discover its qualities and

* From *The Fountainhead* by Ayn Rand, copyright 1943 by The Bobbs-Merrill Company, Inc., reprinted by permission of the publishers.

possibilities, knowing full well that all we can do is to re-
arrange it, not really change it. If we want to know and to
relate and to live, we should skip all abstract questions about
the center of our being, or the goal of our lives, and simply
order the matter around us and in us. Fairy tales about God
and creation or judgment and eternal life are only bother-
some. Only what we can touch is real.

Of course these three possibilities of faith are not the
only ones: the great religions of the earth speak about man's
way to God and how the center of our life has to be brought
into relationship with the perfect God whom we must serve
and satisfy. Each faith is different and some have no gods
at all (for example, Buddhism), but they all offer options
for mastering life and giving it an inner coherence and
equipping man to build his models for all the levels of life
in which he is engaged.

This little book speaks about yet another faith. It is an account of how the mastering of life looks from the perspective
of faith placed in a specific man, who lived long ago in a
corner of the earth, who had very few followers during his
lifetime, who was executed for both religious and political
reasons as an arrogant charlatan, and who died alone. The
man was called Joshua or, later on, Jesus. He belonged to
the working class but became a religious teacher when he
was thirty. He definitely adhered to the Jahveh religion,
which for a long time had been a minority faith among the
Jewish people but which, when he lived, encompassed most
of the Jews.

The story of Jesus' life and death, his teachings and actions, started a movement that is hard to describe. It has
never become the biggest spiritual movement in the world,

but it has spread more widely than any other faith and is found today in virtually all countries of the world. Most of his followers say that his movement is a new religion, but many also say that it is the end of all "religions" and the establishment of a new relationship to all people, to all things, and to God.

One fact about Jesus must be made clear before we start: he is specific. When he speaks of God, he means the God of the Old Testament. Therefore, his message cannot be included with other religious movements. He insists on being himself, and those who come into contact with him have to choose (there is that word again) for him or against him.

This little book speaks about the mastering of life in relation to this man, of whom, by the way, an earlier witness said:

He was not attractive but ugly, and certainly not what we desired. People despised him and even left him to himself. He looked as if in constant pain and he was humiliated. A man people tried to avoid, Yes, he was loathed and got no esteem.

(See Isaiah 53:2, 3.)

CHAPTER TWO

Powers and Principalities

We have decided to talk sense and to look around us before speaking. We talked in a preliminary way. We looked around the arena of this world and saw how diverse and conflicting the interests and hopes of a younger generation are, how many different possibilities are trying to lay siege to us. We saw how difficult it is to take a stand among them that allows us to be engaged in a dialogue with all of them and yet not to submit to any of them. We quickly discovered that to achieve this goal we needed a starting point, a fixed center, a relationship to someone who could give us direction. And we choose—knowing full well that he is only one of the many possibilities—the Messiah of Israel, Jesus of Nazareth.

"RELIGION" AND "GOD"

Those of us who are already baptized, and those of us who were born in homes dedicated to Christ, belonged to him before we were articulate. We all inherit many things from our parents: our nationality, our language, and various elements in our character. There is a definite tradition between parents and children, both of material things and of values. Until we decide for ourselves, we live in this inheritance.

Religion is part of our heritage. A child inherits his religion from his parents and lives with it until he is old enough to decide for himself whether he wants to belong to their religious community. He is then invited to make a decision of faith.

The church has always seen something deeper in this normal hereditary process between parents and children. Christian parents do not have their children baptized simply because the children inherit their faith with their culture, but because they recognize in their children the work of God who is with us in the generations. As surely as life does not stop, but children are being born to us, so surely God renews his relationship with man. New generations are time and time again indications of God's faithfulness to the pact he has with mankind. We are therefore always challenged and arrested by God before we respond in faith. Christianity is not one of those many religions in which men go their different ways to God. Christianity is the story of God coming to man, sharing his earthly life and giving meaning to it. We cannot overemphasize that distinctive quality, and we shall have to come back to it over and over again. The initiative comes from the other side: God's side rather than man's.

Do you understand what the consequences of this point of departure are? Suddenly we can no longer think about Christianity using the categories of general religion. Many people love to do that. They say: "There is only one God, and we all (Christian, Muslim, Buddhist, or whatever) try to serve him, everybody in his own way." Or they say: "Of course there is a great deal of difference among all religions, but in the end they all tell us about the same God."

The Bible is very harsh toward other approaches to God. There are many gods, the Old and New Testaments say, but all except one are idols. People who serve idols are plainly mistaken. There is only one God; his name is made known to Israel; he lived among us in Jesus Christ. The other gods are man-made and void; they have no power; they only serve to satisfy man's own self.

Man can, of course, discover in himself or in nature or in other people that "there is more between heaven and earth" than the immediate reality. He can feel definitely and rightly that something transcends his earthly existence. He may be aware that powers and principalities which he does not control operate in the universe. But these perceptions do not indicate that he has an awareness of the God who is, according to the Bible, the Creator of heaven and earth. On the other hand, he may have no feelings of something else at all, he may not have any religious experiences. He may not notice principalities and powers other than those he can control with science and common sense. Whether a man has had any religious awareness or not, he should not conclude the nonexistence of the God of the Bible. This God makes himself known in definite ways to those who give him the chance. When his initiative breaks into somebody's life, the person has to respond, to decide, and to choose—for or against this God.

Not everybody who says "God" is speaking about the God of the Bible. Adolf Hitler often used the word "God" to indicate the power that was behind his earlier successes. Wars were fought and bloodbaths brought about in the name of "God"—were all these indications of God, indeed indications of our God? The word "God" has lost much of its meaning because people have used it as a noun rather than a name. Therefore some modern theologians think we should not use the word any longer and only speak the name of the God we mean. Let us call him Jahveh as the Jews did, or call him Immanuel as the church has often done. Then be sure about whom you are speaking, and let us not confuse the general religious term with the specific God to whom we are referring. The church baptizes in the name of the Trinity— Father, Son, and Holy Spirit—and with that action it indicates that baptism is not administered merely as a religious initation rite but as a definite claim laid upon a person in the name of that God who became man and who takes us into his company.

JAHVEH AND THE ISRAELITES

The biblical story about this particular God is apparently very simple. It tells about Jahveh, who has a love affair with the world. The story of Jahveh and Israel starts with the patriarchs Abraham, Isaac, and Jacob. Abraham received a mysterious call strong enough to change his entire life—not only his heart, but also his everyday life, socially and politically. A voice lured him away from his home, Ur, and made him a traveling bedouin. This voice identified itself as Jahveh, and Abraham was promised a new land and a great family. That family would be a blessing for all peoples on the earth.

Abraham's call was not an indication that he was about to become God's best friend, but that he was chosen to be a tool, the channel of God's blessing to all other people. Abraham followed the voice and started his pilgrimage without knowing exactly where he would go or where the promised

land would be. He chose to follow Jahveh, however, and
decided to leave his people in Ur. He went in faith.

The second great chapter in the history of Israel and its
dealings with this God is the exodus from Egypt. Abraham's tribe went to Egypt, where it formed a servile minority
under the pharaohs. They worked for the rulers of the Nile,
building their pyramids. Their fate was too harsh for them
to remember the promise with which Abraham had started
his wanderings.

Then the initiative from the other side came again. In
Egypt Jahveh called Moses to liberate the Jews from the
Egyptian oppression, and the pilgrimage started again. The
people hardly had the courage and strength to follow the
voice of their God, but they were miraculously led out from
under the iron fist of the pharaohs. After forty years in the
barren desert, they entered the promised land, a strip of half-
fertile, half-desert country along the Mediterranean Sea.

This story, like the account of the creation, is a tale rather
than an objective historical document in the modern sense.
Again the important elements are the unexpected and sov-
ereign calling of God and the peoples' response in faith. The
children heard the story from their fathers and told it to
their sons in their turn: God has liberated us from Egypt
and destined us to be a blessing to all the peoples of the
earth. This destiny was their central affirmation of belief.

The Jews were never tempted to think that their faith was
only one of many ways to God. They believed that this
strange voice that called Abraham and Moses was unique.
They realized that Jahveh was distinctly different from the
many gods worshiped in the religions of the peoples they
met. They also knew that from time to time this God came

to them, in the words of the prophets, to tell them new and unexpected things.

The Jews made their social and political decisions in response to God. In the course of the following centuries they found that their relationship to God made it necessary for them to write specific laws. They needed to make the structures of their society different from those of the surrounding countries. Yet one can detect a definite similarity between Israel's public life and that of the great powers nearby. This similarity shows that Israel recognized itself as a nation among many nations and connected its destiny with their fate and future.

One of the most interesting points in the Old Testament is that Israel was a stable society. Yet it was flexible and changing because of its belief in God, who was always active. The Old Testament should be read as a book full of tensions between man—who likes stability, security, and conformity—and God—who calls his people again and again toward his future. He encourages the people to change, to readjust, and to trust in him. He urges them to relinquish all their human securities and reaches out to give them a greater security in his love. This relationship with God is the major aspect of Israel's history.

The books of the Bible itself use the terms disobedience and promise. Jahveh promised Israel that he would be with it, bless it, and help it fulfill its destiny to be a blessing to the whole world, if Israel did not bow to idols but did demonstrate actively that God was its Lord. Time and time again, however, Israel was forgetful of the promise. The nation disobeyed the conditions of the pact with God immediately after the escape from Egypt. For that disobedi-

ence God left Israel to its own devices: a small country between the world powers of those days, without help. But the
people of God never disappeared, because the reason for
their existence, that amazing initiative from Jahveh, was outside of themselves.

In Israel's history the first move always comes from God,
and when disobedience is the catchword for the people, faithfulness is the word for their God. His faithfulness does not
mean that he condones Israel's action; it means that he does
not stop attacking their disobedience. He speaks to the people through his prophets, among whom there are princes,
middle class people, and paupers. They have in common
the fact that the urgent voice within them compels them to
speak: words bigger than they are themselves, words that
usually get the prophet into trouble because the people do
not want to hear them, words that have indeed shaped the
course of the world's events.

HOPE FOR THE MESSIAH

However many our uncertainties about the religion of the
Old Testament, this tension between Jahveh and his people
is clear. However we want to explain the history of the
Jewish people, it is clear that trouble was always with them.
A bedouin tribe without a country wandered through the
Middle East, almost disappeared, and reappeared in Egypt
as a colony of slaves under the whip of the pharaohs. It
escaped and wandered for forty years in the deserts between
Egypt and Canaan. For centuries it fought to settle there
and was then overrun by the mighty powers of the north because of its unfortunate relations with another great power
in the south, Egypt. The Persians ransacked the country

and carried the people into exile in two enforced emigration campaigns. A century later a part of the tribe returned and rebuilt its home. Then the Roman Empire ate its way eastward, and Israel became a minor province of the Romans.

Through all these events and catastrophes, Israel remained a people full of hope. Expectation is another way of describing the reality of their faith. Every time the Israelites settled somewhere, they were called away to new adventures. And each time Jahveh disclosed new and unexpected horizons. The old hopes of the fathers were reborn in the living expectations of the children.

The prophets are the ones who coined the central word for this new reality: the kingship of God. Jahveh had always been the real leader of his people. He had led them out of Egypt, he had conducted them through the Red Sea, and he had fed them in the desert. During the first generations in Canaan, an argument had developed as to whether Israel could have a man as head of the community. Did that not mean that God might be forgotten and Israel might once again submit to the eternal temptation to be like all other peoples? If you read the two books of Samuel, you will see that the prophets of those days were nervous about the people's desire for a human king. God is King, the prophets said, and we need no other.

As always in Israel, though, the dialogue on the subject continued. The people remembered that God had always used intermediaries in his dealings with man. Was not Moses a leader of his people, too? And he had never once tried to become king instead of Jahveh. As long as Israel's king represented Jahveh, he would be different from the absolute rulers in the neighboring countries.

Once royalty is introduced the discussion does not stop. The first king, who was the rich and militant farmer Saul, forgot his peculiar calling. He was a good leader, but the voice of Jahveh did not play a great role in his life, and Samuel, the prophet of his day, was not a welcome guest in his palace. Saul even tried to combine the offices of king and prophet and so to extend his rule over both palace and shrine. This grasping for power caused his downfall, and the royal rights went to a very different type: David, the young son of a rich shepherd, a cunning and sly young man, full of tricks, courageous, and popular among the people.

David was certainly no saint in our sense of the word, but during his reign his own character was constantly challenged by the voice of Jahveh. And David listened. Often late, sometimes too late, but he never closed his ears to the words of the prophets. David's reign was the climax of Israel's life as a nation under God.

Later, when life became more difficult and Israel went from catastrophe to catastrophe, the Jews kept expecting a "son of David" to guide them. Even more than waiting for a great man to lead them, they kept hoping for the day when Jahveh would take over the leadership of Israel visibly and totally. Then the kingship of God would be established so that all nations could see it. Foreign nations would come to Jerusalem, "the city of David," to learn how to govern and how to live. Exactly how this would happen the Jews did not know, but the vision of those days was constantly before them. Israel lived for the future, and therefore it dealt with its actual daily problems in the light of that future.

Gradually the prophets understood more and more of the shape and structure of their destiny, and they became convinced that Jahveh would send them a servant of his own, the "anointed ambassador of God, the Messiah." In the writings of the prophets he was only dimly present, and nobody knows exactly what the great prophets Isaiah and Micah meant by their sayings. Sometimes they spoke about the Messiah as the servant, and the servant could take the form of a specific historical figure. But at other times the servant of God was a segment of the people themselves: the faithful remnant who had not fallen for idols but had clung steadfastly to the God who had brought Israel out of Egypt into the promised land.

There is a third possible interpretation of their Messiah. Sometimes the prophets saw the servant of God as a man who would come one day, and then the kingdom of God would break into this world. Strangely enough, the figure of the servant of God was never seen as a great, powerful individual. He was a man like others, an empty man who would be filled neither with his own wishes nor with the aspirations of Israel, but with the spirit of Jahveh. In a way, he would be like father Abraham, always obedient and always on the move. In a way he would be like Moses, a leader but always ready to die in the place of the people. In a way he would be like David, a man among men, but chosen for service and willing to listen constantly to the unique voice. He would be like all of Israel, a combination of all its hopes and visions. He would be the true Israel, and with him the kingship of Jahveh would be established. Therefore he would also be known to all the nations, because in him the old promise to Abraham would become flesh and blood. And he would probably share the fate of the prophets before him: he would be popular for a short time, then he would be rejected, and maybe he would be killed.

Between the time of the Old Testament and that of the New lie approximately two hundred years. In those centuries the beliefs of the prophets took on fantastic forms. The figure of the servant of God, sometimes called "the man" (in Aramaic, "Son of man"), became almost what we would call a hero of science fiction. Something of that idea of the man is to be found in the book of Daniel (written about 165 B.C.), and that idea was interpreted and extended in many other books, some profound, some farfetched. These books were never included in either the canon of the Old Testament or in the Bible.

It was clear, however, that the Jews expected the kingship of God to come through the ministry of the Messiah, and that this messianic ministry would change the world. They never clearly defined what they meant by the term "Messiah." Some expected a political leader who would free the land from the Romans; others expected a purely religious leader who would "soften the heart of the people" so that they would once again become visibly the people of God; a third group expected a renaissance of the conservative attitude of the Old Testament tradition.

Around the year 1 B.C. Israel was full of ascetics, people who through a life of spiritual discipline hoped to hasten the day of the Lord; visionaries, who looked to the clouds for a sign of that great day; zealots, who had the weapons lying at home to start the ultimate revolt against the idol-worshiping Romans; Pharisees, the strong lay movement keeping the law almost overzealously in the belief that the

Messiah would come when Israel kept the law faultlessly for one full day; Sadducees, the intellectuals of the day, eager to translate the Jewish cultural and spiritual riches into the languages of the surrounding Greek and Roman cultures; fanatics of all sorts who had small groups of followers and who, rejected by Romans or Jews, often ended their short lives on the gallows or in oblivion.

The young generation of that day was, as we are, tossed among many possibilities and powers soliciting their commitment. There were the Romans and the underground fighting the Romans. There were the extreme Jewish nationalists and the Sadducees. There were the tax collectors, who lived well under the foreign power, and the guerrillas in the mountains of Galilee; there were the law-abiding and conservative Pharisees and the modern rabbis in Jerusalem. To whom should they commit their lives? Which ideology should they choose?

THE STORY OF CHRIST

The life of the Messiah has been described in several ways. The earliest written documents are the letters of Paul. When he wrote, the stories now to be found in the Gospels were known and perhaps written, but the versions we have in our Bible are younger than Paul's Epistles. The stories about Jesus were safely kept in the memory of the eleven disciples who survived Judas, the traitor. They had told the stories again and again. Since probably none of them could read or write, they used the trained mind and memory of the illiterate, keeping the stories alive and unviolated in an oral tradition. Paul wrote on the basis of these stories. He was concerned to show the relevance of the good tidings Jesus

POWERS AND PRINCIPALITIES   39

had brought to all people and their relation to all problems of life.

In committing himself to the way of Jesus, Paul traveled a lonely road, for Jesus was widely rejected in his day. The Nazarene's early popularity with the crowds, largely due to a strange authority and the miracles he was reputed to do, had dwindled quickly when people discovered the cost of total commitment to him. They were puzzled by the strange combination of suffering and victory in his words. The strange combination of stern judgment and total forgiveness in Jesus left them unable to rely on the traditional system with which they had lived.

Jesus had identified himself with the central figure of Israel's hope. He had taken the prophecies of Isaiah and Micah and Daniel, and said: "I am the Son of man, the remnant of Israel, the Messiah." When it became clear that a choice for Jesus involved a break with the religious leaders of Israel, the people started leaving him. A break with the religious leaders meant an eventual split from the whole accepted Jewish community because Jesus insisted that his concept of *agape* (love) and *koinonia* (fellowship) included call-girls and collaborators with the Romans. His community included Romans and Jews, saints and criminals, terrorists and fellow travelers with the Roman aggressor. The new community of Jesus robbed the Jewish people of all their carefully built securities.

When he died, there were only eleven close friends left. The story, told by these eleven men and a handful of women around them, that he was seen again and had talked to them, was hardly believed. People became interested again only when they discovered that this small community had a dif-

ferent way of life, of handling the powers of life, a different
economy, different attitudes to politics (they refused to be
nationalists like the rest), and a very different religion—if
you could call it a religion at all. Some even went so far as
to choose this new life of freedom, or this new life in Christ
as some of the friends of Jesus called it. Their commitment
to Christ changed their outlook on life completely.

From this perspective Paul wrote his letters. Most Christian literature was and is written in keeping with that commitment.

The following pages, too!

POWERS AND PRINCIPALITIES
AS PAUL SAW THEM

Paul often writes of powers, principalities, rulers, thrones,
dominions. We find them in his letters to the Romans
(8:38 f), 1 Corinthians (2:8; 15:24-26), Ephesians
(1:20 f; 2:1 f; 3:10; 6:12), Colossians (1:16; 2:15). For
a long time the church thought that the Apostle was referring to primitive religious concepts, and people paid little
attention to what he said. As with so many things in the
Bible, whole centuries can pass before people notice certain
points.

What Are the Powers?

The interpretation of these words began to change first in
Germany. The change started after World War I, when the
word "power" took on new meaning. Until that time power
had meant something invisible and metaphysical; now it began to take on concrete meaning as the word was applied to
nations and their striking forces.

We continue to speak about the powers, meaning political realities. During the last years an even wider use of the word has become common: Powers can stand for the impersonal rulers of our society—economy, propaganda, sex, public opinion, religious sentiments, racial prejudice, nationalism, or colonialism, all those things that undoubtedly exist in, influence, and sometimes dominate our lives without ever being fully visible.

Consider, for example, the powers behind the scenes in plans to help developing countries. The West has spent billions of dollars in these programs, but the inequality between the haves and the have-nots is growing rather than diminishing. Suprapersonal powers are at work, which make it impossible to act quickly and decisively. Colonialism and nationalism, inflation and oversaturated markets suddenly start playing a role. Education, and even a sense of history, differing among different people, become powers that prevent an equitable distribution of wealth.

You can go on and on with this subject. Consider relations between parents and children. In many countries, although not in all, there is a real problem involved. If you ask the parents what is wrong, they will start by blaming the children. If you ask the children, they will blame the parents. "They don't want to understand us!" both groups say. There seems to be some almost "demonic" power that drives parents and children away from each other. "Something" makes it very hard to talk together, forcing both parents and children into loneliness.

In France and Germany many books have been published with letters from teen-agers and young adults. It is fascinating to see what they say about such things as parent-child relationships. I quote from a French girl's letter to her teacher: "I love my father dearly and he loves me. But we cannot talk or discuss without quarrelling. I don't know why, but we are ruled by very different spirits, inherent in our different generations."

A young German student answered a questionnaire: "When I left home [to study] I also left the place where communication with my parents was possible. It seems that since then we belong to a different class or level, I don't know how to explain it more precisely. Maybe we are fighting different battles, with different enemies, and need different powers to assist us in our battle to survive."

Powers and principalities here seem to be very real forces, even if they cannot be easily defined. German theologians discovered that these strange words Paul uses are highly relevant; so they started to look into what Paul means by them. What they found was exciting and indeed relevant for their own situation. They discovered that when Paul discussed powers, he was relating the gospel of Jesus Christ to the way the Christian faces these suprapersonal and sometimes subhuman powers. We all have to make our peace with these forces, or we have to fight them.

When Paul chose the rejected carpenter of Nazareth, he knew that he must completely reorder his life and thought. He knew that this relation to Jesus was not meant to be a spiritual affair that would change only his heart and his Sunday morning schedule. This commitment would revolutionize all his life: his political thoughts, his social convictions, his relations to other people. Only through radical change in his way of living and thinking could he know that his relation to God had altered.

Now let us turn to the Bible. We will take one specific case in which Paul writes to a congregation about how the gospel applies to the role and function of the powers in society.

I am aware that there is no agreement among New Testament scholars as to whether the Apostle Paul is the author of the Letter to the Colossians. The prevailing thought is that he is not. The letter was, however, attributed to him by the early Christian community and in that tradition I shall also use the name of Paul for the author of this letter.

Religion in Colossae

Colossae was a little town in Phrygia on the River Lycus, a tributary to the Maeander, which in Turkey is now called the Menderes. There were two other towns nearby: Hierapolis ("Holytown"), famous for its many temples and healing baths, and Laodicea, important for its trade. Colossae, too, had once flourished as a trading town but fell asleep as trade shifted to Laodicea, which was closer to a major Roman road.

Since all these cities were important, or at least had a significant past, people came to them from all over the known world. There were many Jews in the region; they had been forced to live there by a Roman dictator who feared their astute economic sense and strong, peculiar religion. There were Greeks who had brought their own shrines. Ephesus, which was close by, had produced the worship of Artemis, goddess of the moon. The mysterious cult of Cybele, goddess of nature, also originated in Phrygia. Trading Egyptians, a garrison of Romans, and people who had come from the far north and east, completed a complex society in which there was peace for all, provided no group claimed supremacy. The curing baths provided solace for all, and in the end the religious groups of Phrygia found themselves in a pleasant climate of agreement. Everybody had his belief, often based on a nebulous and vague collection of religious concepts.

That world was a bit like our own. Everybody has his beliefs (most of which support what is beneficial for himself, his country, and his business), but underneath there is a vague agreement about the common basis of all religious expressions: God the father of all, and the brotherhood of men. In Colossae this agreement-religion had almost become independent and taken the place of the various beliefs it was derived from. From Paul's letter and some other documents about this "faith of the baths," we can determine some of the major issues in this conglomeration.

The first article of the Colossian faith was that God is holy and unapproachable. He lives in the eternal light and is too holy to be really bothered by the unclean history of mankind. Man is a rather negative creature, imprisoned in his earthly desires and cut off from God. Through his actions, he spoils the little spark of good in him, which aspires to higher life, without much hope of doing better either here, in an afterlife, or in a new life.

There is one other important thing to know. Between God and man live the powers, the angels or the demons, the authorities or principalities, or whatever you want to call them. God rules the world through them. They are his emissaries. This belief was not only held in Phrygia. The same doctrine was also taught in Israel just before Jesus' time. The book of Daniel has a passage about it in which God is represented by an in-between power who fights another demon, the ruler of Persia. (See Dan. 10:4-14.) In the apocalyptic literature (a technical term for cryptic books that reveal both the nature and future of a situation) of the Jews, these beliefs play a considerable role.

The in-between powers are of various sorts. They can be the embodiment of nationalism, so that each region has its "power" or "angel"; they can be religious powers that bind man to certain obligations; they can be (and very often are) powers of nature—the snow-angel, the hail-angel, the thunder-power. Their function was not only to rule the world; they could also help man to liberate his divine spark from the earthly prison. If man was able to pacify and satisfy the in-between realm of angels, demons, and the like, he might be able to return to his creator, and his soul would be where God is. Religion in Colossae was therefore interested only in the in-between realm. Many ways were indicated whereby man could satisfy the angels. Asceticism and mysticism were the most popular.

Asceticism means exercise in self-control and denotes a way of life in which all unnecessary ways of satisfying the senses are cut out. The extreme form is embodied in the fakir who not only takes a minimum of food (which should taste badly lest it stimulate the senses!) and a minimum of sleep, but also hurts his own body in order to humble the flesh. Asceticism in some form is found in all religions and originates in the assumption that our spirit is the divine spark, imprisoned in our body and our senses, which are evil in nature.

In Phrygia, asceticism could have come from various sources. The Jews, as we learned recently, had ascetic sects just as the Greeks and the Indians did. In all cases it was believed that some of the in-between powers and principalities could only be satisfied and softened toward man if strong asceticism were practiced. Even more important was the belief that this way of life could restore the original divinity of the soul!

Mysticism was practiced in Paul's day through the mystery religions. The worshiper was introduced into a secret ritual, which could involve anything from hypnotism to fraternity meals, and he became part of the cult for a certain god or goddess who in turn favored him during his life. The participants knew the secrets of certain old hymns and names of categories of angels. There were complicated philosophical systems, speculating about the origin and essence of life, the nature of sin and death. By so classifying them they would be able to understand the real knowledge (*gnosis*) and be able to live profitably and responsibly. This knowledge involved power.

Christians in Colossae

The small Christian community of Colossae, built up by Paul's collaborator Epaphras, had great trouble in not drifting away on the mainstream of the prevailing religious life. Was it not all perfectly respectable? Was not God holy and silent and far away? And could man, as he was, ever reach out for God, even please him, without going through something like this religious strife? Was it not true that Jesus spoke about the flesh opposing the spirit? Should not, therefore, the Christian community be even stricter about the pleasures of the flesh than other religious groups?

What about these powers? Could not a child perceive that there was more in this life than just human beings? How exactly should Christians behave toward these powers? Submit to them, fight them, pacify them?

In the early Christian settlements (and perhaps in those of the future?) a lack of churches was normal, as it is now in many parts of Asia and Africa, and increasingly in Eastern Europe. Small communities, surrounded by hostility, struggled to exist. In such a tense situation faith became something different from faith simply acquired at home, in which one grew up without ever having to face decisions. We must realize that for the Colossians this commitment was difficult to fulfill. They knew very well that they were not Christians for their own benefit, but that God had called them there for service to their fellowmen. They were there to testify to the exciting story of Jahveh and his relationship with the Jews first and now also with all men. They were bearers of the good tidings that man had been reconciled to God through Jesus' death, and that through Jesus man could enter the world where the gifts of God could be realized.

How do you deliver this message when you are twenty people in a city of tens of thousands? How do you live that new life, demonstrating God's love for men, when you are such a small minority? Of course there were Colossian Christians who said that they should not even try. They should simply be humble people, walking with their God, trying to live as inoffensively as possible and putting the emphasis of their life on the safeguarding of the truth. If they mingled too much with the pagans and their strange beliefs, they would certainly lapse into the colorless faith prevalent in the town and simply be another fragment of the whole religious picture!

How much like many Christians today, who argue that the world is both bad and strong and that therefore the church should be primarily the safeguard of the truth in Christ—that repenting men may enter into the house of the Lord with holy hands. Politics and social business are important, but not for the church! The church is a ghetto, a walled-in place where holiness is practiced. Asceticism is not so bad after all. Let us not mingle with the evil people outside.

Thousands of congregations all over the world isolate their religion. This sort of Christianity has made Jesus Lord of the church and the devil lord of the world. All the powers in this world are trying to lure us into apostasy. A cry has gone up from the younger generation in the church saying that for them isolation is the prevailing heresy in the church. The church, they said, is interested in our souls, but not in us ourselves, not in our political decisions, not in our attempts to help build the nations in which we live.

Some Christians—whether in Colossae or in our countries today—adopt another attitude. They say: "Listen, we are not here for ourselves, we are here for the others. Therefore, we have to live where they live and help them achieve their goals." Such were those Colossian Christians who gladly worshiped with non-Christians, saying: "There is some truth in what you say. We have many similar goals so we must work together."

In Eastern Europe there are a few Christians who have no criticism of communism whatsoever, and who hail the present regime as faultless and entirely pleasing to God. In the West many people think and believe that our Western way of life is exactly what God wants, and they are willing to risk a war to defend what they regard as the absolute truth. They applaud when political candidates pay lip service to religious values, even when the content of these remarks is as vague as the beliefs of the Colossians. In Africa there are Christians who have totally accepted a policy of white supremacy. Some people have swallowed the concept of nationalism in the new states as the real Christian emphasis in politics.

In some countries the Christian churches are large and powerful. In others they are in the position of the church of the New Testament, small and outwardly powerless. Despite the difference in size, they are both exactly like the church in the town of Colossae. The German scholars at the beginning of this century were wise when they suggested that the words Paul used for the powers are much more up-to-date than we thought! Behind these words there looms a world that looks at the same time very different from ours and almost painfully like it.

How Paul Communicated

Before we look into what Paul wants to say to his bewildered friends in Colossae (whom he had never seen personally), we should examine his style. It is interesting to note that Paul uses the very expressions of the people he is addressing. Yes, even whole phrases come out of that religious jargon. He often uses the Greek word *pleroma,* which meant, in the common language of Colossae, the fullness of God and the final goal of all human attempts to find God, whether through asceticism or through mysticism. He speaks about concentrating "on things that are above" (Col. 3:2, RSV) and about the powers that exist between God and men.

For the Jews who spoke about angels and powers, these words often stood for spirits who influenced life on earth, mainly nature and politics. Paul, however, does not seem to be very interested in the personified powers. In the letter to the church in Rome Paul says: "For I am sure that neither death, nor life, nor angels, nor principalities, nor things present, nor things to come, nor powers, nor height, nor depth, nor anything else in all creation, will be able to separate us from the love of God in Christ Jesus our Lord." (Rom. 8:38, 39, RSV) For the Jewish scholar of angels and powers that was a peculiar list: death, life, height, depth, time, and the powers. All these forces were clearly very earthly and could apparently dominate our lives so much that the love of Jesus could not reach us.

In the First Letter to the Corinthians Paul says: "Whether Paul or Apollos or Cephas or the world or life or death or the present or future, all are yours." (1 Cor. 3:22, RSV) Here, although the words for powers are not directly used, Paul is clearly speaking about realities that, for the most part, are invisible but which dominated the life of the congregation in Corinth.

In the same letter Paul says: "None of the rulers of this age understood this [the hidden wisdom of God]; for if they had, they would not have crucified the Lord of glory." (1 Cor. 2:8, RSV) New Testament scholars agree that the rulers are not simply Pilate and the Jewish high priest, but the powers that lay behind these men and made them act as they did: religion and the state, pre-eminently.

In the letter to the congregation at Colossae, we must read a few texts:

Be on your guard; do not let your minds be captured by hollow and delusive speculations, based on traditions of man-made teaching and centered on the elemental spirits [the powers] of the world and not on Christ. . . . He discarded the cosmic powers and authorities like a garment; he made a public spectacle of them and led them as captives in his triumphal procession.

Allow no one therefore to take you to task about what you eat or drink, or over the observance of festival, new moon, or sabbath. These are no more than a shadow of what was to come; the solid reality is Christ's. . . .

Did you not die with Christ and pass beyond reach of the elemental spirits [powers] of the world? Then why behave as though you were still living the life of the world? Why let people dictate to you: "Do not handle this, do not taste that, do not touch the other"—all of them things that must perish as soon as they are used? That is to follow merely human injunctions and teaching.

Col. 2:8, 15-17, 20-22, NEB

Here again the powers are forces that shape life in Colossae. They are public opinion and the pressure of conformity, moral rules and religious observances, philosophies and ideologies. For Paul the powers make up the structure of life in which the Colossians live. In the Letter to the Galatians, the Jewish law fulfills the same function as a power between God and men, which dominates and often enslaves the people who are subject to it. They are at the mercy of these powers.

Paul had a very subtle concept of the powers, which he offered to the congregation in Colossae.

Paul's Letter to the Colossians

The way to be free from the powers is simply through Jesus Christ. That looks, at first sight, like a bad preacher's remark. It makes us feel as though we were in church, where the minister works for ten minutes on the analysis of a problem and then gladly announces in the last two minutes that the answer to the whole problem is Jesus Christ. But that is not what Paul is doing. He is far from giving an easy answer. He sweeps away the whole realm of the in-between powers and says bluntly: "The only power between man and God is Jesus of Nazareth."

In the first chapter of the letter to Colossae we read, in my own translation:

If you, Christians in Colossae, ask *who* will be able to rescue you from that domain of darkness the people in your city talk about, or *who* could release you so that you can get back to God, or *who* could forgive you your sins which, as they say in your city, keep us away from God, my answer is God, who did that through no other power than Jesus of Nazareth. If you are looking for the image of God, it is Jesus; if you, with your mystery religions, want to learn who is the Prince of all things, it is Jesus! If you are trying to find out who was the instrument of creation, it was Jesus! And as far as the visible and invisible things are concerned, and all that stuff about orders and thrones, sovereignties, authorities, and powers, let me answer you once and for all: The whole universe was created through Jesus Christ! Still looking for what was there before all other things existed? The answer is Jesus. Want to know whether there is a system in this universe that keeps things together? Jesus is that system! Jesus is also head of the church, which is his body. He—not some angel—is the origin of the church. He was also the first to return from the dead, and is supreme in all things, Jesus alone. The *pleroma* of God—the fullness, the totality, the very nature of God—is not in your soul's little divine spark, or in some angels between God and man: It is only to be seen and to be had in Jesus Christ.

Col. 1:13-20

Therefore Paul says a bit farther on in that same chapter: "It is him whom we proclaim, and him alone." (See Col. 1:28.)

Do you see what Paul tells these poor religious people around the Christian community? He does not say: What you teach is rubbish! He does not deny that God is holy and that somehow the contact between God and men was broken. He does not even deny that there is an in-between level through which men have to come back to God. He does fill these different thoughts and constructions with one simple name: Jesus of Nazareth.

Even more important, Paul does not say that man has to come to God through all kinds of religious rites, but he emphasizes that God has already come to man in his Son. The whole religion of Phrygia is attacked and destroyed. It had been built entirely on the pious attempts of the people to restore their relation with God by themselves. Then came Paul, saying: "It is *God* who reconciled *you* to him, not you who reconciled yourselves to God. And God did that through his Son, Jesus Christ."

God's grace is made clear in Paul's letter to the Colossians (as I have translated it):

Through Jesus, God chose to reconcile the whole universe to himself, through the shedding of his blood upon the cross, through him alone! Therefore mystery religions are sheer nonsense. God is not so complicated that we have to go through all kinds of machinations. God came very close to us in his Son. It suffices to accept him as the one who was "the initiative from the other side!" Therefore, ascetic exercises are not necessary to "kill" the flesh. God has broken open the prison himself, by coming in himself and breaking the locks from the inside.

(See Col. 1:20.)

When we speak of the mission of the church to the world, we are referring to God's reaching out to us. Our mission to the world is our participation in God's mission, in which we play a secondary part. We tell others what God has already done for them and us: he has reconciled the whole world to himself.

The Powers and Creation

In this process of ascribing all reality and its origin to Jesus, there is one phrase that we should look at more closely, because it is of great importance for our subject:

In him everything in heaven and on earth was created, not only things visible but also the invisible orders of thrones, sovereignties, authorities, and powers: the whole universe has been created through him and for him.

Col. 1:16, NEB

In other words, the powers, whatever they may be, were created by and for Jesus of Nazareth. That is an important insight, because it means that the powers are not evil, as many people think. They are not created by the devil, who cannot create anyway, but by God himself, and they are meant to be the skeleton of the world in which we live. We all know from experience that these powers form a framework for our lives. Our lives are by no means logical reactions to our own desires and wishes, nor are they the clear combination of the success our work deserves and punishment for our mistakes. Life is ten times more complicated! In our lives there are powers at work that we master only with difficulty and of which we are often unaware.

When one travels in Africa and meets young people in the newly formed states, it is clear that all of them are in the grip of nationalism. That is not necessarily bad. Nationalism only becomes dangerous and wrong when it enslaves us to such an extent that we cannot criticize our own land any longer. It is dangerous when we assume that everything our country does is good and that everything which will strengthen and glorify it should be supported, even when it is bad for other countries and other peoples. In the new nations the younger generation is often close to that assumption, and few among them are really able to see that nationalism is a two-faced power.

I took Africa as an example, but what about our own lands? Is the United States or Great Britain or the Netherlands much better? When someone from abroad criticizes our land, we may feel constrained to defend it even when the critic is right. That is even more clearly true when, for instance, a Communist criticizes the West. Before we allow ourselves time to think through his critique, we are in the middle of an emotional defense of our ideology. There the power of nationalism shows its power over us. Even in small things the strength of this power shows. When somebody behaves differently from us, even in small matters, we get nervous and often judge him for being different. In my university, for instance, one really could not wear a bow tie. There were traditions in Utrecht—"man-made teachings" Paul would call them—which became such powers that our dress was regulated by the customs of man. Do you not know examples of traditions that control behavior in your own surroundings? Powers that once had a positive function quickly become tyrants that enslave us.

Paul says that these powers were created by God. Without them life would be impossible. How could we live without time, for instance? Would not society at once be in chaos if there were no way to measure days and nights, hours and minutes? What would happen if there were no morality or no law? Life would be chaos. Paul knows that, and he speaks strongly about all these structures as God-given, created by and for Jesus. Those last four words are still a bit difficult to understand. We must look at them, both in the context of the Colossian beliefs and of Paul's knowledge of the Christ event.

The Colossians were looking for the origin of all creation and for the system that gives order to the universe. They had built an elaborate system of angels and powers that had been instrumental in the creation and which, with God's blessing, had ordered life on our globe. Paul says in Colossians 1:17 that all things are held together in Jesus Christ. The Greek word he used has the same root as our word "system." So to the speculators Paul says: Christ is the system of creation. For him and by him all things were created.

In the total understanding of the work of Jesus Christ, Paul referred to him as the source of all things. Paul knew that however the beginnings of life actually took place, they could not have come about without Christ, who spans all human life. In both the Old and New Testaments, the followers of the God of the Jews simply attributed the beginnings of this life to their Lord, rather than trying to explain precisely what happened. The Old Testament story of creation came into being when the Jews discovered that surrounding peoples told tales about the beginning of the world that did not take Jahveh into account. That was blasphemy to them, so they pondered how Jahveh had been involved in it all.

In the New Testament a similar thing happened. When Paul is faced with other beliefs about creation, he knows one thing deeply and certainly: Whatever happened could not take place without Jesus Christ. All things were created by him and for him. He is the system of creation.

Paul uses strong language, and the intention is unmistakable: we should never let ourselves be brought to worship the powers or be defeated by them, because they are created by Christ and therefore subject to Christ. Why be afraid of created things? God, who was there in the beginning, is stronger than they are. We should look to him for help and for an understanding of the powers rather than going to the powers themselves.

The Powers After the Fall

Once we have seen that God through Christ is the source of all creation, we must face the problem of evil. Its entrance into the creation and all its attractiveness have been mysteries from the beginning of time.

We have learned in the last decades that the first chapters of Genesis should not be read as stories describing different historical periods. The beginning of Genesis is an explanation of the world as it is today and as it is claimed for Jahveh. It is not the description of the beginning of life but of its origin. It also tells the reason why our own existence is both glorious and beastly. We Europeans saw six million Jews carried away to their death and did not do what was in our power to prevent it. We saw the lie of Nazism reign. We saw incredibly egotistic wars to keep our colonies for ourselves. Most recently, we tortured and killed in North Africa. We Europeans know how deep-seated the mystery of evil is in our lives, not only as individuals but also as peoples.

Americans, especially white Americans, fully confront this power of evil now that they are under attack from their Negro fellow citizens and from the peoples of Latin America who accuse North Americans of economic colonialism.

Human history is a beastly tradition, but it is still not without glory. The achievements of man, especially in the last hundred years, are magnificent. We print, engineer, discover. We change the surface of the earth and are sailing through space; we are definitely gaining ground in our battle for health and life. We are pulling ourselves out of the fate our forefathers unquestioningly accepted as being the fate that God had planned for man.

The history of man is a glorious affair. Yet we are not able to divide our riches adequately; we live in luxury while many people starve. The battle against illiteracy, unemployment, hunger, and disease in many parts of the world is not going well. The history of man is a puzzling affair. This mysterious combination of victory and defeat, of right and wrong, of glory and perversion is explained to us in the first chapters of Genesis. God created us gloriously, but we became corrupted; since then we have been egotists, trying to be independent of God, challenged by him, longing for him, and disobeying him all at the same time.

The powers, the structures in which we live, share the mystery of good and evil. Although created as instruments to keep order in the world, they began to dominate rather than serve man. We no longer know them as friendly agents of order but, in their horrifying form, as rulers of men. When Paul, in the Letter to the Romans, asserts that the powers cannot divide us from the love of Christ, he clearly indicates that the powers would like to estrange us from the love with which God reaches out to man.

Paul discusses, in the Letter to the Galatians, the relation between Christians and the Jewish law. He makes it clear that once "you were the slaves of beings which in their nature are no gods," (Gal. 4:8, NEB) but which apparently set themselves up to be gods and put themselves between God and men. While, through the mystery of evil, men often become subhuman, so that they do not even reach up to the standards of humanity, the powers become gods rather than instruments. In both cases, of the powers and of men, they become separated from God and so miss their calling as servants.

This separation does not mean that either men or the powers are evil in themselves. Man is a strange mixture of evil and good, each fighting for control of his life. So also with the powers. They keep the creation from becoming mere chaos, but they also prevent man from communing directly with God or his fellowmen. What would a high school be like without the specific customs it has acquired during its existence, without order, without authority, without strong personalities, or without some degree of conformity or group spirit? Still, these forces can easily develop into evil powers, which separate the student from parents, from students in other schools, from students in other parts of the world who are educated under different academic systems and various philosophies.

Professor Hendrikus Berkhof tells in *Christ and the Powers* about the powers that operated in Germany in 1937 as Hitler took over the country. The German people were positively drawn towards Hitler and his ideology because his rule brought back law and order; the society that had almost collapsed during the years of the great crisis started to function again. At the same time the powers got out of hand and became the most gruesome slave drivers the people had ever known. It was indeed a tragic example of how powers, which in themselves were helpful instruments, became demons and gods when made independent.

A much more controversial example of the presence of good and evil together is the missionary movement of the churches in Asia and Africa. We will speak about missionary work again later, but it also needs to be mentioned in this context. The missionary movement has brought untold blessings to these two continents. The gospel liberated Asians and Africans from the powers of darkness, the ignorance and fear present in pagan religions with their taboos and idols. The gifts of medicine and education were especially valuable. The independence of most Asian and African states is inconceivable without the influence of the Christian mission. Therefore, we must be careful about criticizing that splendid piece of our history; no criticism can start without a prevailing emphasis on the value of the missionary activity of our churches and the Christians who often gave their lives for it.

At the same time, we cannot be deaf to the critique that arises within the countries themselves. The missionary movement in many cases has become a power structure that dominates the very people it once liberated. Today the missionary has a hard time. He is often accused of colonialism and domination. Education and medical science, intellect and learning, and often even the color of his skin become masters rather than servants. So even the purest religious motivation can still be corrupted into the worship of powers that have set themselves up as gods. No wonder Paul had such an interest in them! Paul's picture of these principalities—which were created as servant structures but which, through the mystery of evil, became independent half-gods—needs further careful exploring.

The Cross and the Powers

The center of Paul's teaching is undoubtedly the certainty that on the cross Jesus overpowered the powers. When Jesus is crucified, two things simultaneously become clear: It is the powers that bring Jesus to the cross, and it is Jesus who defeats the powers. You remember that Paul said: "If the rulers of this age (that is, the powers) had understood the hidden wisdom of God they would not have crucified the Lord of Glory. But since they did not understand it, they indeed tried to do away with him." (See 1 Cor. 2:8.)

We now also understand why the powers fought against Christ. Jesus had come as their Lord, in him they were created, and in him they met their master. Since they had become independent, however, and had set themselves up as gods, they could only attack Jesus. Their service structure had become a structure of domination: Neither politics nor religion was helping men to live according to God's will any longer. On the contrary, they enslaved men to a new servitude, which was the opposite of the freedom God had wanted for men. Jesus had to put them in their place, whether or not they wanted to acknowledge him as master.

Jesus' task is expressed in the Letter to the Colossians, in the passage: ". . . he [God] has made you alive with Christ. For he has forgiven us all our sins; he has cancelled the bond which pledged us to the decrees of the law. It stood against us, but he has set it aside, nailing it to the cross. On that cross he discarded the cosmic powers and authorities like a garment; he made a public spectacle of them and led them as captives in his triumphal procession!" (Col. 2:13-15, NEB)

This is not an easy text, but we can understand it in relation to the rest of Paul's explanation of the gospel. The usual explanation of Jesus' death on the cross is connected with sin, guilt, and forgiveness. Although our rebellion separated us from God, Christ has taken our guilt and sin on himself and died our death. God has recognized this role of intermediary and accepted his sacrifice as sufficient for all mankind.

In our text Paul discusses the same reality of Christ's sacrifice, but he looks at it from a different perspective. The Apostle is interested here mainly in what the cross means in relation to the reign of the powers. That he is still referring to the same event is made clear in the words: "For he has forgiven us all our sins." Paul points out that what Christ has done on the cross is not only to take our sins upon himself, but also to liberate us from the tyranny of the powers.

When he speaks about the decrees of the law, he employs the same Greek words that he uses to discuss the man-made regulations. (See Col. 2:20.) In both instances the word used is "dogma." These teachings about what we ought to eat and what we ought not to eat, what we should touch and what we should not touch are the "human injunctions and teachings" that have become barriers between God and man. (See Col. 2:21.) Paul is speaking about Moses' explanation of the law, in which the law is not the manifestation of God's mercy for man but has become a tyrant standing between God and man. By the death of Jesus on the cross and in his resurrection afterwards (these two must always be seen as one indivisible event) the powers of death and guilt, and the slavery of man to these powers, were broken.

where they belong, to the function of service rather than
nation.

owers Dethroned

us look briefly at the powers that Paul says have been
owered and see how Christ's victory affected the daily
the Colossians.

interesting that the first power Paul sees as being de-
d is religion, for religion had become a tyrant. In
ians 2:16 Paul tells his friends that nobody is to take
ristians to task about what they eat and drink, or
e observance of religious days, be they pagan (fes-
nd new moon feasts) or be they within the realm of
religion (the Sabbath). This must have been quite
oversial point. Paul continues by saying that people
rticipate in self-mortification and angel worship, and
ho boast about their visions, are all religious ego-
o use their experiences and observances as a means
spiritual authority over others.

ms to me that the Apostle here underlines what he
tten elsewhere. The Christian community has only
, the person of Christ himself. The church is called
both the freedom to eat and drink and the freedom
t and drink. In Paul's days the eating matter was
portant than the drinking matter. The issue involved
ificial meat that was destined for use in the pagan
Afterwards it was often sold for domestic use.
Christian eat meat that had been consecrated to
any people said no, for so doing would link the
some way to the cult of Cybele or Artemis. Non-
ys Paul, let everyone make up his own mind. We

Until the coming of Jesus on earth the powers were never recognized in their rebellion. But when God became man and the powers set out to kill him, the true state of their enmity against God was brought out into the open. On the cross the powers were exposed and made into a public spectacle. It seems that all the powers of the earth were assembled to kill Jesus: The God-given law became an idol that led to the condemnation of the Son of God. The political authority—which, in the words of Jesus, only had power because God gives it (see John 19:11)—signed the execution order of the Son of God; the piety that had originated as a response to the great deeds of God in Israel became the hysteria that drove the people to insist on his death. The powers were forced to commit themselves in this ultimate encounter, and they chose to commit themselves against God.

The other phrase Paul uses to denote what happened in the event of the cross is "to lead them as captives in his triumphal procession." This image comes from a custom of the Roman army. When a Roman general had subdued another nation, the rulers of that nation had to march into Rome on their bare feet, behind the chariot on which the conqueror rode. The image used here is a dramatic one. The cross is not only the sign of defeat for Christ, it is also his chariot of glory. It is the high altar on which Jesus presents himself as the living sacrifice for all men, accepted by God. It is the place where "all is fulfilled," where Jesus triumphs over the evil powers which had kept us away from God for so long and which now have to see that Jesus carries away the sin of the world. The cross is the final place where the battle is fought.

There had been countless meetings between Jesus and the powers. Herod had tried to kill him when he was an infant; in the desert, at the beginning of his ministry, there had been the direct temptations of the evil one; during his ministry the demons and the powers had fought him, or rather had fled from him, and now finally they must see that he meets death. But death means the certainty of the resurrection. The Son of man must suffer, but in three days he will rise again. The powers cannot withstand such a blow, and so they are humbled behind that strange chariot of victory which they themselves had built.

The final phrase used for the confrontation between Jesus and the powers on the cross is that "he discarded [the powers] like a garment." (Col. 2:15, NEB) The text is difficult here, and different translations are possible. The verb is clear enough: It means to strip someone of his clothes or of his arms. Paul says that what Christ did on the cross was to strip the powers of their would-be divinity. It should be observed that the action of the cross does not destroy the powers: It only puts them in their place. It robs them of the absolute authority they should not have taken in the first place; they become Christ's servants again, fulfilling the purpose for which they had been created.

The subjection of the powers is the most important part of Paul's argument, and therefore of ours. On the cross the powers were cut down to size. Jesus showed that their function was not intended to be one of domination and independence. That position could lead to nothing but enmity toward God himself; indeed it did end in the tragedy of Christ being executed by the powers that were "created in him and for him." But with the resurrection the powers are over-

powered. They have met the stronge
brought back to where they belong—
of victory, serving him and subject t
the powers have been restored to th
event of the death and resurrection
dangerous masters, they have become
ination structures, they have becom

We must always say, when we tr
lical story, that although the victor
effects still have to be made visib
masked, they are exposed and de
yet brought under the feet of Jesu
goes on. In his First Letter to the
about the day when Christ will tur
Father, "after abolishing every kin
and power. For he is destined to
enemies under his feet." (1 Cor.

What has happened on the cro
and time again. The church also
powers. Paul makes that clear
the Colossians, where the rule fo
Col. 3:5-4:6.) The words used
should do, now that we know
powered, are the same as thos
the cross. We are invited to bind
of glory; we are urged to make

Paul's conception of the po
but a revolutionary and practi
not only as an account of our
but also as a command to go
under his feet. We should not

should demonstrate our freedom rather than our fear of idols! Paul does not tell people to eat or not to eat, but insists that they are free and therefore not to be forced to either a negative or a positive decision. It is a sign of the Christian community that people are free to do either and still live with each other in love.

Paul also teaches the Christians to be free in the observance of holy days. The church is not bound to observe certain days because some are holier than others. Both the pagan festivals and the Jewish Sabbath are feasts given to man so that he may enjoy himself and remember the reason the feasts were instituted. No observance of holy days should be allowed to enslave people. If the Sabbath is a day on which we are slaves of observance rather than celebrants, do not observe it. If the Christian community wants to take Sunday for its observance of the resurrection of Christ and not the Sabbath, let it! If Christians want to meet on Friday and not on Sunday, let them! The important thing is that the congregation meets, not when it does so, how often, or where.

Asceticism should likewise be practiced in freedom rather than from a sense of obligation. When people say that in order to belong to Jesus Christ we have to indulge in all kinds of self-mortification, like fasting and an extremely sober way of life, they have become subject to the power of self-mortification and have lost their freedom in Christ. But since we have died with Christ, and the powers have no hold upon us any longer, we are free. Of course we may fast, of course we may live a sober life, but in freedom and not as a requirement for belonging to God's new people. The only requirement for belonging to God's new people is to join with Christ himself. He is the solid reality, and all the other things mankind has devised to keep us close to him are but shadows. They are allowed to help us, but they are not allowed to dominate us!

Our real task is to kill the idolatry that makes us witness against the freedom God has given to us. The worst we can do to Christ is to continue to worship the powers and be slaves to them. Paul mentions all kinds of social wrongs like indecency, greed, anger, passion, cursing, and lies. They are all indications that we are not free and are not really able to master the powers, but that they have a hold on us, forcing us to follow and obey them.

Sex is intended to be our servant. But when it leads us to uncontrolled expressions such as lust, fornication, and indecency, Paul detects that slavery to the powers is real. He sees slavery to the powers when our indignation turns into anger, passion, and revenge. (See Col. 3:8.) He points out our slavery to powers when we have to tell lies because we do not master truth any longer. We are called to freedom, and its expressions are compassion, kindness, humility, and patience. (See Col. 3:12.)

In this letter Paul does not explain freedom in other areas of life, but in the last chapter we shall see that he outlines the way for a free mastering of life.

A SUMMING UP

The theme for this book is mission in unity. Have we wandered or are we ready to understand these words in a new way?

Our argument ran as follows: There is a mission of God toward the world. It starts with Abraham, is continued in Israel, and reaches its climax in the birth, life, death, and resurrection of Jesus. The theme of this mission is that God wants this earth to be full of his love and his justice. This initiative comes solely from God; man is only the recipient and invitee. There is one element of this initiative that does not only deal with persons but with suprapersonal powers, the structures of our societies with all their influence on our lives. These powers were created as service structures to keep order against chaos, to give us measurements of time and space to live by, and to equip us with intelligence to keep it all functioning. Yet they have become gods and enslave men, who now are suddenly surrounded by negative commandments rather than freedom to deal positively with the structures of order.

The evil nature of the powers became clear when God himself became man; the powers tried to put him aside and finally crucified him. They thus gave proof of their rebellion against God. But Jesus, in reconciling them to the Father on the cross, put them back where they belonged, namely in his own victory parade, where they are openly recognizable as servants rather than masters.

The task of the church is simply to join Christ in his power struggle, not making the powers our enemies but recognizing them as runaway horses that must be controlled. This task is apparently done by three activities: by unmasking them publicly, by stripping them of their semi-divinity, and by humbling them by Christ's victory.

In the last two chapters we will see exactly what that means.

CHAPTER THREE

Our Powers: Servants or Masters?

It is always fascinating to discover that Bible study is much less "religious" and much more practical than we ever thought. Behind those heavy biblical words that seem to come from another world (and as a matter of fact they do: we do not live in the Middle East!) there is a living reality. In order to find this vital reality we must keep studying the text to find out what it wants to say. Bible study is one of the ways by which we realize that God, when he came to be one of us, did indeed give us enough wisdom to live by for all centuries to come. This does not mean that all we have to do is look in the Bible to find an answer to all our questions or that the answers in the Bible apply to all times. The Bible gives us an unsurpassed cross section of the human reaction to a unique God, who does not want to be searched for but who does the searching himself.

At the same time, the Bible, by its very style and content, forces us to be serious about the world in which we live. Take the example of the Letter to the Colossians. Paul writes it in the jargon of the religious people of that town to make sure that they understand him. That means that he studied their religions intensely in order to communicate to them. We must do the same: We cannot understand what

Paul wants to say if we do not study our own world. What a farce it would be if we studied all the specific powers Paul was talking about and prepared ourselves to unmask those powers, which in actual fact have already been unmasked! The powers of our own time would then have a free hand among us. For example, there was a theologian who wrote a long book about the holy wars of the Christians against the Turks, while his own land was being invaded by the Nazis.

If we want to understand Paul's attack on the semidivine powers of his day, we shall have to take into account that he says in the same letter: "And when this letter is read among you, see that it is also read to the congregation at Laodicea. . . ." (Col. 4:16, NEB) Paul's letter is written for a specific group of Christians, but others should read it as well. We are like the Laodiceans, and like them we shall have to apply the letter to our own specific situation.

THE TWO-FACED POWERS OF OUR DAY

What we shall do in the next pages is discuss a few of the great powers that try to enslave the whole world and our whole younger generation. But you who read this book will have to do the same homework, examining the large and small powers that exist right on your doorstep and that try to enslave you and your community. What is written in the following pages may not apply to you. If not, you must remember that you belong to the same church as your generation in other parts of the world. Knowing others' questions is not only helpful when similar questions come to you but is also a simple and self-evident requirement of sharing the same baptism.

Complexity

Let us say quickly that there are many powers at work in our world. It will not do to mention just two or three and think that all powers can be included in those categories. In fact, would not the first power to mention be the *complexity* of our situation? By complexity we mean that life can no longer be described in easy formulas. The different communities in which we participate and the different roles we have to play complicate our lives. A complex situation develops after a process of differentiation has been started. Differentiation simply means that all social groups, social institutions, and social interests become more and more specialized. This leads to the formation of new groups and interests.

Scientists today have a hard time. There are professors of theoretical mathematics who are not able to control the work of their own students any longer. Differentiation has come to all of us, and that means that most of us have to operate on many levels at the same time.

Let us take one example of differentiation. In Holland there is a little village, with perhaps nine hundred or a thousand inhabitants. All the people know each other by name; all know the relationships among the others; all know the professions of the male inhabitants of the village. There is one pattern of behavior; you can follow it or not, but if you do not, you are clearly cutting yourself off from the community. The leadership of the village is in the hands of several people: the mayor (that is a profession in my country), the rich farmers, the minister, the teacher, and maybe the local lawyer.

Now a large industry picks our village as the location for a new plant. Two or three large factory buildings are erected, four thousand new workers are brought in, and new houses, roads, a shopping center, and even a railroad are built. The process of differentiation begins. A few farmhands' sons hear that the plant pays better wages than the farmers do, so they go to work in industry. They enter a community in which they do not know other people. Soon they discover that the relation between the generations is different here. An older man is not a wiser man who should be honored for his years —on the contrary, he is a somewhat slower worker and is therefore replaced by a much younger man. The behavior toward the old men in the plant is different from the behavior toward their grandfathers or their fathers' friends.

Then they get more money and learn from their comrades that money is not to be saved, but to be spent. So they buy a car or a motorcycle, and suddenly the world opens up; they start traveling and seeing cities. Their lives have changed. Their work takes place in the plant and cannot be discussed in the marketplace any longer.

The political system changes because suddenly the class distinction becomes apparent. They vote left-wing Labor; their political views probably cause tension at home. The little village has become a microcosm of society at large. Behavior toward older people at home is different from behavior toward older people at work, new scales of authority arise, new conflicts have to be faced. Each individual plays many roles, and the integration of these roles becomes a continuous battle. This complexity is clearly a power in our time. It is able to change people's lives and has even changed the life of some continents.

The question is whether complexity is a servant or a master. If we are honest, both aspects are there. Of course we have benefited greatly from differentiation. It means a widening of our horizons, and we all recognize the value of that. Few people in our time would rather have lived in the Middle Ages or even a hundred years ago. Specialization and complexity have given us the opportunity of choosing between different careers, different styles of life, and different ways of building up our own personality. The upsurge of industry (which is a child and a parent of differentiation at the same time) in the so-called developing nations is a clear indication that people have recognized that these powers serve us, and they want them to serve their countries as well. Cars, medical developments, pocket books, electric razors, hair dryers, and an overwhelming choice of products are only possible because of never-ceasing differentiation in our world.

The old established society, which has been forever abolished, was not a paradise either. The village community was not only a socially integrated culture; it was also a prison from which one could never escape and in which the shackles of slander and mutual observation allowed little freedom for the individual. The process of rapid social change, which is another name for the process of differentiation, has given millions of people all over the world a new sense of dignity, has brought them economic welfare and social well-being. People who were hungry have acquired bread, and people without any rights—because the authorities were so firmly defined—have started to organize themselves politically and to take their own share in responsible government. Differentiation is clearly a servant structure for mankind.

But the value of differentiation as a social structure is only one side of the picture. The report of the World Council of Churches' Conference on Rapid Social Change, which was held in Thessalonica, Greece, in 1959, shows the other side, which is equally true. It points out the profound effect of social change on human personality.

Men must pay a price for the revolutions involved. . . . The price is seen in "lostness," loneliness, frustration and disillusionment; in the family, between the generations, between employers and employees, between country and town, between different tribes and races that confront each other in the multitribal, multiracial communities, created by the demands of expanding industry and commerce. . . . Men and women are also asked to suffer.*

To see the truth of this statement, we only need to look around us. Read a book about young people in big cities, who have come to find work and to share in the riches of the urban concentration. Go to see a film about the loneliness of modern man, who has lots of people around him but very little community. Look at the slums, which rise up around all the big cities of the world. Observe the terrific tensions between tribes and races in Africa and North America.

Differentiation is two-faced, as all powers are. It is clearly meant to serve us. It succeeds by making it possible for us to live the life we want, helping us to conquer nature, and helping us to become both individuals and members of a community. But all the time it works for us, it also tries to enslave us, to make us lonely, to make us animals in a herd.

* *Dilemmas and Opportunities,* Report of an International Ecumenical Study Conference (Geneva, 1959), pp. 8, 9.

Social change involves complicated processes in which we are but a small factor. The farmer, however hard he works, is subjected passively to price fluctuations; the worker, however good he is, may find himself without a job because of economic developments he can neither control nor understand.

The domination of the power of differentiation can become so strong that some people can only rebel, and juvenile delinquency and the multiplication of gangs start to worry society. The juvenile delinquent has more than a negative function in society. Instead of being only a destructive animal, he is first of all a watchdog whose barking indicates that the powers have got out of control. Our attempts to understand, help, and cure him should be preceded by gratefulness as much as worry.

Some people may lose all their interest in the possible change in the pattern of authority and stop thinking about their own involvement in politics or economics. Thus, the search for some measure of integration of all the different facets of the modern society may lead to dictatorship, either of one party or of one group in society (those who have the capital, for instance), or indeed of one person. Slavery may be the result of the process of differentiation, which in the beginning was the process by which we were liberated from another type of slavery.

Do you see what Paul meant when he wrote to the Colossians about powers that are both created and perverted? This old piece of theology written in the first century of our era has not lost its relevance. In the next chapter we shall see the significance of Christ's invitation for us to share his mission to bring the powers back to their proper place.

Secularization

When we look at the process of differentiation from the point of view of the church, we speak about secularization. This is the development in which all sections of society, which were once under the guidance of theology, have become independent and secular (that is, not sacred). We all remember from our history classes that once, in the Middle Ages, theology was not only the queen of the sciences but also provided the context for all human activity. The theologians were the scholars and some of them, as theologians, were interested in medicine, education, law, natural science, political science. There was no man who had not first studied his share of theology before he moved into other academic fields.

Perhaps the best example of such a dogmatic approach to science can be seen in the Communist countries. Here all spheres of life are subject to the ideology of the party; all scholars—be they psychologists, physicists, or educators—have to work within the categories as explained by the official interpreters of the party's ideology. Many people make the mistake of thinking that the Communist countries are the most secularized. They are wrong. The Communist countries are the only ones left where a "sacred" ideology provides the context and control for everything, as it did in the Middle Ages in Europe.

If we look at the picture of the twentieth century in the West, however, we see a different scene. All the sections of society that were once controlled by theology have broken away from it and have become independent sections of the community. In many places theology is still a partner in the discussion on how these different levels of our life should be arranged, but there are places where theology is ignored. Instead of the dogmatic control of the medieval church, only the subject itself and the researchers determine the limits and the content of present scientific study and action.

The monologue of theology, in which the eternal truth was handed down, has changed into an ongoing conversation among all partners involved in the search for the answers to men's questions. For example, there was a time in which the law was simply given by the king with the blessing of the church. Punishment was given according to the letter of the law, and there was always a theological reason behind it. The accused was condemned without a significant defense and certainly without a discussion of the sentence he deserved. Today the measure of the punishment is decided by a series of discussions which involve the defense, the law (represented by the judge), the jury, the psychiatrist, the accused himself, and perhaps social workers and ministers of religion. The law is not given by king and church, but is developed from continual conversation among many people in the land. The laws in the countries of the West are flexible and relative. The same flexibility can be found in other segments of modern society.

What happened? First of all there was a slow development in theology that discovered the essential message of the gospel to be that man is free. He does not need to be subject to the powers, not even to the power of theology. Man is given the charge to subdue nature, and he is free to choose his own methods. There is no reason why he should not explore the universe or the atom. The Bible does not give us an all-encompassing plan for this activity. On the contrary, the Bible, in its account of God's dealing with man, gives us full freedom to deal with the world. There is no Christian science, and there is no Christian politics; there are only Christians engaged in science and Christians engaged in politics. Those Christians who have their community in the church will, communally and personally, live out their faith by confronting the subject with which they are dealing together with non-Christians who are working on the same problems.

It took theology a long time to recognize this freedom. The late Middle Ages are colored by long and agonizing fights between those who defended the right for free scientific and political action, in the name of the freedom of the gospel, and those who denied the other group those rights, in the name of theology as queen and tutor of all sciences. The fight continues today. The church and theology are still suspicious when science produces new discoveries and theories about the creation of life out of nonliving matter, about the evolution of man from lower species, about the existence of other universes.

Once again, we encounter a double-faced power. The process of secularization is clearly a blessing for both the church and the world. It is a blessing because it liberates the church from a function that was not intended to be hers in the first place. The church engages in theology to make the gospel understandable to man, to make sure that no false beliefs flourish in the Christian community and to give a basis for its preaching and its confessing function in society. Theology is not meant to produce a domination structure that would rob man of his freedom to think or to explore. On the contrary, the theologian, if faithful to the gospel, would uphold such rights with all his energy and further them as well. The church, which preaches the Lordship of Christ and invites people to join him and them in Christ's own mission to the world, cannot dominate or force people into belief. To do so would deny the heart of the gospel, which says that man encounters the living God and is challenged by him to decide whether to accept or reject this involvement in mission.

Secularization is also a blessing because, in practice, the domination of theology over secular affairs has made church history a shameful chain of heresy trials, lost battles with scientists, and ugly involvement in the political power struggles. This history made it impossible for many inside and outside its own community to see that the church is a servant to the world, as its Master is a servant to the world.

Was the church, then, entirely at fault when it resisted secularization? No, because secularization was not only a servant of mankind, bringing him freedom, but it was also a new master, forbidding man to be really free. The servant called secularization can easily become the god called secularism. All "isms" indicate enslavement, including this one. Secularism is a philosophical school that requires men to give up living in encounter with God, and makes a new dogma (in the sense of man-made teaching, as St. Paul uses the word in Colossians) out of the historical process of secularization. Man must believe in science and progress; he must witness to the fact that all that science does is good and is pure.

The church soon saw the danger of science turning man from God and, therefore, fought the scientists. Granted the tactics of the church were dubious, the scientists deserved some opposition. It is one thing to say that our forefathers were monkeys, and quite another to say that God therefore did not create the universe. Both scientists and theologians had trouble with that combination. Many scientists said: "Man originates from the monkeys, and therefore God cannot have created him." Many theologians said: "God has created man, and therefore he cannot have originated from the monkeys." If you remember what we have said about the creation stories in the Old and New Testaments, you know that this is a false alternative.

Another way in which secularization influenced the church was that it forced the church to become just a religious community. Since all the controls of the church over society were removed one by one, the church did not see the role it had to play in a changing world; it often became merely an association for religious exercises. Of course the church is not necessarily isolated from the rest of society: when it is liberated from control over the world, it can start to serve the people. Yet for some time both the secularists and the theologians cooperated in making the church just one more community in our world, a group that had religion as its special concern.

You know that the gospel dies when it is taken out of the world. It becomes just another religion, just another road for men to go to God. But the gospel is the story of God coming into this wild, changing world of ours and the invitation for us to join God in his mission. If the result of secularization is that the church cannot serve the whole world any longer, then secularization has become a god in itself, an independent power that requires the worship and submission of the people.

Academic Grades

Let us look at a few other powers around us today.

I was once teaching religion in a high school and made some good contacts with a few of the students. One day a boy came to me during the break to tell me that he had lost the struggle with one of the powers. Of course he did not say it that way, but he was troubled and had the feeling that somewhere he was failing to master his life. In the beginning, he said, everything in school was fine. He participated in the life of the school, he had many friends and felt part of the community. But then, two years later, the question of his future began to press on him. He knew that he would need a scholarship to go to college; and in order to qualify for a good scholarship he had to "make the grade."

From then on the "grade power" had him in its control. He had to cut out participation in the life of the school to a great extent; he had no time left to play with his friends, let alone to help somebody who was lagging behind in his work. Slowly he felt that he dropped out of the community and became a lonely individual who had only one object in life—to "make the grade." He was puzzled, because he remembered how positively he had begun on this road, and how gradually he began to feel oppressed and indeed enslaved. Was he wrong?

Community Spirit

There is a power we might call community spirit. As a servant it looks like the power that enables us to live together. In a complex society such as ours we need close cooperation and a team spirit in order to be able to integrate the different levels on which our community exists. Our industrial age requires the cooperation of all those who are engaged in production. The scientific enterprise, especially in regard to the natural sciences, would be impossible without the teams and expert groups who contribute to the penetration of nature. Schools and governments require people who are willing to give their contribution to a greater enterprise, and who are willing to listen and to discuss rather than deliver monologues. Of course, our whole education in the modern world is based on the denominator of the team. We know that team spirit today is no longer the mark of a real sportsman, but that it has become the absolute necessity for our civilization.

The power that enables us to mold our individual souls for the good of the whole is called team spirit. There is no doubt that it is essentially a positive force in our lives. There are countless stories about the power of team spirit saving and transforming people's lives.

The other face of the power of team spirit is conformity, which, if described in general terms by the people who are the chief agents in promoting it, sounds exactly like team spirit. It, too, includes the gift of being able to work with other people, but it always has the overtone of "the group, which of course must decide." Conformity turns people into puppets who sharply and obediently react to impulses that come from the outside, and who are afraid of initiative and even more of being different from the others. While team spirit liberates us from loneliness and ineffectiveness, conformity enslaves us to the will of others. I remember a girl who played the flute very well, but who would not think of telling anybody because the guitar was the popular instru-

ment of the moment. Team spirit invites an ongoing discussion between the members; it tries to make the worries of
one the worries of all. Conformity kills any discussion, because it may make us say the wrong thing, which may not
be appreciated and, what is even worse, may be remembered. Conformity—to the neighborhood, to the mob, to the
social class, to the professional group—is a terrible power
in our time, one that is certainly well known in America

Channels of Communication

There is a power called mass media. By this term we mean
all channels of communication—be they paperbacks, newspapers, movies, or television.

Again the double character of the power is written in
large capitals. Mass media have opened the world for us.
We participate in historical events in other continents. Even
the evaluation of these events reaches us through the written
word and through news commentators almost the same day.
Compare for a minute our involvement in world affairs with
that of three generations ago. What did our great-grandfathers know about the world? They had read books about
it, but there was no immediate contact; while we, when eating our popcorn with one eye on the TV, have the world on
our kitchen table. When President Kennedy was assassinated,
the whole world from Iceland to South Africa sat by their
radio sets and TV screens and were with the people of the
United States, united in an immediate and profound sor-
row. There is no excuse for the generation now growing up
to say that they have not seen what it means to be a refugee
or hungry or involved in war. We all see it daily and have to
live with it. The mass media are precious to our culture;

they liberate us from ignorance and educate us to take our share of responsibility.

But we are in danger when this power gets out of hand and produces propaganda instead of news. Propaganda can be defined in several ways. You may call it "directed or guided news" or "unchecked indoctrination," but whatever you call it, an element of enslavement is always present. If propaganda is selected news—which means that only bad things are told about the enemy and only good things about yourself and your country—people who read or hear or see this kind of information are deliberately weakened in their judgment. Again, propaganda does not treat people as persons, but only as voters or as rebels or as uncritical supporters of the propaganda machine.

Propaganda is undemocratic because it deprives people of the chance to make up their own minds and decide accordingly. When we hear the word propaganda, we think of countries other than our own; for us the word has associations with Communist countries like Russia and China, or fascist dictatorships like Spain and Portugal. But the power of propaganda does not need a police state to back it up. If a free country in the Western world produces newspapers, TV programs, films, and books that distort the news by always selecting the bad stories about the adversary, it produces propaganda and enslaves people.

Anyone who has traveled in Eastern Europe knows that people have many criticisms of their governments, but it is hardly true that the people are terribly unhappy. When the Russian cosmonauts circled the earth and returned safely, the crowds in Moscow were bigger and more enthusiastic than the American crowds that met to greet their astronauts.

We must remember that behind the iron curtain there is a large group of people who have chosen a socialist development of their countries rather than a restoration of the situation as it was before the war.

Propaganda exists in all human communities. The big difference between a democracy and a dictatorship is that in the democracy the people have access to correcting material if they look for it, but in a dictatorship they have not. But in both cases propaganda is a power that requires worship of itself and acts like an uncontrolled, independent, semi-divine perversion of the mass media. If we take a bird's-eye-view of the world, we see that millions and millions of people in both democratic countries and dictatorships are enslaved by it.

Race

We need not say much about the power of race; not because it is unimportant, but because more and better material about it exists.

Race as a positive power contributes to the diversity of mankind. Paul speaks, in another context, about the many-colored wisdom of God. (See Eph. 3:10.) The different races on our globe show something of that wisdom. The Bible is not interested in racial differences. For God all people are alike, and biological and cultural diversities are unimportant in the light of the story of God becoming man.

As soon as the power of race enslaves man, however, it becomes very dangerous. It divides people along unnatural lines and sets up power blocks which have little to do with the problems of survival and life on our planet. When race is recognized as a power, it blows itself up to an almost insurmountable problem, causing bitterness and strife and using people's energy that should have been used in better ways. The sooner mankind realizes that the racial problem is much more a social and ethnic problem than a race problem, and so begins to overpower that power, the better it will be.

Sex

A beautiful example of the two-faced nature of the powers is to be seen in the power of sex. From the delight of Adam over Eve, to the ecstasy of the man and the woman rejoicing over each other in the Song of Songs, to art of modern times, man has known that no lovelier power than sex was given to serve him. The delight a man takes in a woman, or a girl takes in a boy, or an elderly couple reserve for each other is hardly matched by anything else. We know that God smiles on a relationship between man and woman, since in both the Old Testament and the New Testament the fellowship between Jahveh and his people is again and again movingly expressed in the language of the encounter of the sexes.

And yet when sex becomes man's slave driver, so that he involuntarily has to subject himself to its service, misery can follow. There is no stronger tie than the sexual one and no stronger destructive power than this same sexual power. Freud explained that most of man's creative and destructive powers are related to his sexual drives. We do not have to believe all that Freud writes in order to see the truth behind that statement.

For a younger generation, the question of mastering life is always closely related to the mastering of the power of sex. The Germans call it the "royal test of education." For that reason it is always necessary to direct a major part of our attention to the sexual question and the conversion of sex from a domination structure into a service structure. It is not good to try to destroy this power, as some of our ancestors have done; nor should we let it rule our lives. The power of sex must be confronted, like the other powers, with the victory of Christ that enables us to bring it back to where it belongs: in the category of a servant of man.

Religion

What did Paul have in mind when he warned the Colossians against the power of religion? Was he simply speaking about "other religions"? Apparently not. The people who take others to task over what they should eat or drink, or over the observance of the festivals and the Sabbath, are apparently Christian members of the congregation, just like those who advocate "self-mortification and angel worship." Is Paul warning the Colossians against those who introduce elements from other religions into the Christian congregation? Or is Paul saying that religion is one power among the others and, therefore, must be kept in its place as servant structure?

We all know that religion is a power. In the history of man there is an awesome chapter on how, in various cultures, different religions have kept people together in the face of bitter calamities. Wars have been won because of the inner coherence of the religious convictions of the soldiers. Karl Marx once said that religion is the opiate of the people. He meant that the masses of his day were kept drugged by the promise of eternal life, which made them passively endure the oppression of the capitalists. What he was really saying was what Paul said: religion is a power. As such it can be either a drug or an incentive.

Is what Marx said true of Christianity? To a large extent, yes; he should, however, have been more careful with that little word "is." It can easily be argued against Marx that no force in the world has been more revolutionary than Christianity. The freedom the gospel preaches, the commandment to cultivate the earth, the commandment to preach the gospel to the ends of the earth, the incentive to love one's neighbor, have indeed often been violated and used to drug people into a false complacency. On the other hand, they have produced revolutionary forces in a way that nothing else has. Many philosophers and political scientists have told us that even communism itself, in some strange way, is a product of Christianity.

Religion indeed enslaves people, but not the fellowship that is a communal and personal relationship to the God who —contrary to all other gods—leads his people into the world, not just to heaven. The question is whether such a relationship, or such a complex of relationships, should still be called a religion. There are many theologians today who would rather not use that word for the Christian gospel and the Christian community, because it does not recognize the unique character of Christianity and makes it only one way of worshiping God in the midst of many other possible religions. Christianity is then reduced to one way in which "the religious spirit" is channeled for mankind.

All those religious forces that set themselves up between God and man betray religion rather than helping man to hear God call him into the world. They make it difficult for man to distinguish what God really wants him to do. Especially dangerous are religious forces that set themselves up between Christians and other people—as if we were really different, or better, or more loved.

When Sunday becomes an end in itself, in which we "have to go to church" or "have to go to the youth group," these religious activities have become masters and they oppose Christ. When the rule for the new life that Christ gave us in the commandment to love and serve becomes a morality in which Christians are forbidden to do this, that, and the other, the gospel has been made into a power that robs us of our freedom. When Christian doctrine stops being a servant that helps us to communicate or explain our faith and becomes something to which people must submit themselves, that Christian doctrine has become a domination structure and should be exposed.

If one form of church organization stops helping the church to be an effective witness of the gospel to the world, but is still being imposed on people as the only God-given structure, this form of organization has become a power that sets itself up independently and, as such, against God. When a denomination becomes a power in itself, concentrating on its own heritage of doctrine, order, or worship rather than on "the solid reality which is Christ's," this denomination, or this particular confession, has become a semidivine power and needs to be dethroned. In short, all religious activities, teachings, and ministries that are manmade, and that allow Christians to be anything more or less than people who share God's mission to the world, are enemies of God, and Christ will ultimately bring them under his feet.

THE POWERS AS MASTERS

How, then, do we know when the powers have become domination structures? What does it mean to dethrone them? When do we know that the powers have transgressed their limits and have themselves become gods? For example, how could the Germans have known that Hitler was not the bringer of order and economic welfare, but that he was being used by the powers—or was using them to institute a barbarian dictatorship through which millions would perish?

Those are questions that must be answered if we are to be able to master our lives. Of course, they do not necessarily have to be answered in well-phrased theses. Answers often come in the form of clarifying questions or through indications of where the answer may lie. We should understand that not having the right answers does not help us to avoid the wrong ones. Let us list a few such clarifying questions, which have been produced by the Christian community during the ages.

The first question is whether the recognition of powers as domination structures should take place in the whole church. That is to say, not only in the younger generation or in a national church or in a group of national churches, but in the whole church of Christ around the world. Is it not very difficult, for instance, for the churches in South Africa to see the right way of living with the racial powers? They need the help of churches that are not so emotionally involved and may therefore be more objective. Is this not also true for the churches in North America in relation to the political powers at work in Latin America? People have an almost mysterious faculty for recognizing demons in other houses, but regarding those at home as friends even when they are subject to them.

Most South African whites do not know that they are slaves of the political powers that make them suppress their black compatriots. Many North Americans do not recognize the positive character of the powers in the bitter struggle for social and economic change which the Latin Americans have to fight—and often have to fight in the face of opposition from the United States.

Recognizing our relationship to the whole church involves a number of concrete tasks. For one, it requires us to take our common baptism seriously. We realize that we are not to fight the powers, but that in dying with Christ (our baptism stands for that reality) we are dead to the powers already and they have no chance to enslave us.

In principle our baptism eliminates the fight, not the tension, between the generations. Baptism is our ordination as Christians. Baptism involves us in the full mission and life of the church. We are part of the whole company.

Of course, as always in the church, we have to become what we are. What we receive are promises, and what we are asked to do is to work them out effectively. Our efforts are certainly important in strengthening the relation between the generations.

Baptism does not only bring a new unity with the older generation, it also brings the realization of unity with all the church. Our struggle with the powers becomes a common affair of all Christians. This endeavor is not only an inter-denominational one in which the churches cooperate, but an ecumenical one in which the churches, acting together, seek to join in the mission of God in the world.

RECOGNIZING THE POWERS

The struggle with the powers, being the struggle of the whole church, is also the task and the privilege of each gathering of Christians and of each individual. Within Christianity it is hard to distinguish between the individual and his community. In a way, the Bible tells us that a man can only become fully a person when he enters the fellowship of the people of God. A man can only really learn what it is to live in a community when he knows that God knows his personal name and his heart. (See Luke 16:15.) To answer the call of Christ means to enter his community, to be put in the right context. To be a Christian in isolation is a contradiction in terms. "Only in prison or in extreme loneliness," said Dietrich Bonhoeffer, the German martyr, "will God visit us in our loneliness; the normal channel of his presence is the community." How, then, can the Christian community recognize the perversion of the powers?

I feel that Paul, in his Letter to the Colossians, gives us a whole series of concepts that equip us to discern when a power cuts itself loose from its servant function and sets itself up as an idol to be worshiped.

To Divide or Unite

First, we have to look closely to see whether the powers divide or unite. If they are created and given to serve us, their original task can only be to unite, because unity belongs to the essence of creation. The Christian church over the centuries has tried to explain and underline this unity in a number of ways.

The most important doctrine is the mystery of the Trinity, in which we confess that in God there is a perfect unity between the Father, the Son, and the Holy Spirit. We may not understand this doctrine—how could we?—but we must realize that our whole Christian life is acted out under the invocation of the Trinity. With this confession we are baptized and buried; we begin and end our worship services with it. Again, we know and understand very little about the nature of God, but we all agree that he himself is the giver and mystery of life. In the Bible we are taught that the mystery of life is one of diversity in unity. All powers submitting to God must therefore unite.

All the powers Paul has been speaking about and those we have recognized on the basis of his teaching are uniting powers in their essential nature. Let us take the example of the nation. There we have a unity symbol of the first order. It unites individuals, classes, races, families, and tribes. It does not kill individuality or diversity within the country, but brings them together in a productive tension. However, when the nation is perverted into accepting an ideology of nationalism, the united power of the nation is not productive any longer, but becomes destructive. Country turns against country. History teaches us that only a catastrophe can be the end if the power of nationalism is not overpowered and checked.

Here also we will say something about the powers that have divided the Christian church. Many of the ugly divisions within Christianity started as positive powers of renewal. A group or an individual discovered an element of the gospel that was neglected in the church, and a renewal movement started. Then, often mysteriously, the power of renewal became a dividing force. Those who were trying to renew and reform often divided themselves from the other members of the church. Sometimes a church that was only interested in the maintenance of the old forms and beliefs refused to recognize the servant function of the renewal movement and made itself into a domination structure. The result was a division in the church and another scandal in the world, where the name of the Lord was blasphemed because of the way the Christians lived.

Today most of the churches have recognized this evil of separation and have learned to say that all divisions in the church, however beautifully they started, are contrary to God's will. Understanding the origin of barriers, we shall be much more on the alert to recognize which powers do divide the church and which contribute to the manifestation of its unity. Paul, in the letter we are looking at, says clearly that the renewal of the church breaks down the divisions between "Greek and Jew, circumcised and uncircumcised, barbarian, Scythian, slave, freeman." (Col. 3:11, RSV) Everything that builds up these differences is contrary to God's will.

To Focus on Ourselves or Others

Powers become perverted powers when they cause people to concentrate on themselves rather than on Christ, who is the head. (See Col. 2:19.) The same thought appears a few verses later when Paul says that we have to lay aside all ruthless greed. (See Col. 3:5.) Greed also is an attempt to make ourselves the center of the universe. Powers were meant to be servant structures and to enable us to live not for ourselves but for others. In Paul's letter he is clearly speaking about the Christian community and relationships among Christians. There we have to watch out for a concentration on our own needs and gifts. How often it happens in our churches that people look down on others who are not equally religious, or do not have a faith that is as strong as theirs. They behave condescendingly toward those who do not come to church regularly, who do not contribute enough money to charity, who do not come to the youth group, who do not participate in prayer meetings or the Sunday church school. These activities, which may be helpful elements in individual lives, are turned into rules for the conduct of others.

Paul warns us against imposing our ways on others. He is not, it seems, impressed by people who see visions, or who perform serious exercises of self-mortification, or who have beautiful theological theories that they use to criticize others. Paul knows that the gospel turns people's attention away from themselves and toward others. He knows that religious exercises are largely concentrated on *myself* and God. Paul puts his faith in the gospel that concentrates on others. Wherever the church sees powers that turn people inward, away from others, it recognizes idols.

All powers that take our attention away from the Christ whose concern is with all people are against him. In its attempt to discern the powers and their functions, the church must look closely to see whether all powers are directed toward Christ, that is, toward others! Focusing upon Christ, the head, means giving close attention to the world and its needs, because his mission is solely directed toward that!

To Be Worshiped or Be Used

The church must, in the third place, watch to see whether the powers allow people to worship them. When that happens we know we are face to face with a rebellious power.

Here we can think of the personality cult as we know it in politics. When a political leader allows people to worship him, he is no longer the servant of his people, but has become their idol. When he becomes dominating and self-centered, he is no longer a political leader but an enemy of the people he is leading. Politicians these days often seem to forget that. That fact seems to me extremely dangerous, not only for the people involved, but also for politics as such.

Prosperity is another good power. It means that people can live a life of dignity and peace; they can have joy and well-being; children can benefit from prolonged education; the sick can be cared for; and old people can feel secure. Housing becomes decent, and the possibilities for recreation are expanded. There is enough to eat and enough to wear. Art flourishes and people can enjoy music and books.

The power of prosperity is perverted as soon as prosperity becomes an idol, and people take the attitude of the rich man in the gospel who said: " 'Man, you have plenty of good things laid by, enough for many years; take life easy, eat, drink, and enjoy yourself!' " (Luke 12:19, NEB) The power is corrupted because it becomes an end in itself. People forget to share their riches with others; they forget God because they do not need him any longer; and they start to believe that riches can solve all problems and are sufficient to live by. They become slaves of affluence; they worship it as the essence of their life; before they know it their main object in life is to defend their luxury.

Our Western societies are in great danger of becoming worshipers of their wealth. We have become greedy, and all of our help to the poorer part of the world does not come close to repaying what we earn from those countries. When other countries require their share of the pie, we react furiously to defend our wealth as if it were the greatest good in life.

The fact that people can worship the state, sex, money, a certain ideology, even a creed or the founder of a denomination, becomes obvious when they are unable to criticize these powers and, instead, become defensive about them.

To Sow Enmity or Reconciliation

Further, Paul is quick to point out that the perverted powers cause enmity rather than reconciliation. (See Col. 3:8.) The power of mass media, corrupted into propaganda, is put at the disposal of the powers of enmity. The power of economy, perverted into the power of economic pressure, causes people to indulge in "anger, passion, malice, cursing and filthy talk" (Col. 3:8, NEB) rather than in compassion and friendliness or forgiveness. (See Col. 3:12, 13.) All these powers, used to cause or to prolong hatred in the world, have the clear marks of rebellion against God and his creation.

To Bring Loneliness or Fellowship

Again, the perverted powers cause loneliness rather than fellowship. One of the strongest examples here is the power of sex. Created to serve man in his most intimate relationships, sex creates almost intolerable loneliness when it becomes a master. True, the sex pervert is lonely, but even lonelier is the person who has reduced all his relationships to sex. We all know marriages that were entered into because people were attracted to each other sexually, in which the partners never bothered much about the totality of their relationship. Sex in their lives became the one and only power binding them together, with the effect that other areas of life had no chance to develop. The one power indeed dominated them to the exclusion of all others.

Sex, taken out of its context of serving man, becomes a source of egotism and, therefore, of loneliness. We all recognize that sex is one of the strongest powers, and that it has laid seige to our society more than any other. The church will have to be sure to keep it continually under surveillance. The church will need to treat sex both joyously and cautiously without either being afraid of it or careless about the questions it raises.

To Imprison or Free

Powers that have transgressed their servant function cannot liberate men any longer. They make fanatics out of people and imprison them in their ideology. Wherever fanatics are created, the powers have succeeded in becoming gods. We must therefore be attentive to Paul's emphasis on the freedom of those who are in Christ when they deal with the powers. "Do not let your minds be captured," he says. (Col. 2:8, NEB) You have passed beyond the reach of these elementary spirits. (See Col. 2:20.) Christ is our liberator. Still, the powers try to bind us.

The race issue may be a good example. Discussion of this question is everywhere shot through with emotion: feelings become more important than facts. People allow themselves to be guided by sentiment and fear rather than by facts and hope. In such a setting a solution is very difficult to find.

Take South Africa, for instance. Five different groups—

Afrikaans-speaking whites, English-speaking whites, Negroes, coloreds, and Asians—are now living apart in "apartheid." Within the Dutch Reformed Church in South Africa a debate is going on about the possibility of these five groups living together in peace. The debate is a new phenomenon. Until recently the Dutch Reformed Church stood solidly behind the government. But within the past few years, the situation has changed. Other churches from the outside have recognized perverted powers in South Africa and have pointed them out to their brethren in the country. A steadily growing group of ministers and laymen have recognized that something has gone wrong in South Africa.

A large part of the white population, however, is now the slave of fear and prejudice to such an extent that they are deaf to any of the solutions posed to them by their white compatriots. "Communists," they shout, when someone dares to criticize the government, as if the only opposition to Dr. Verwoerd, Prime Minister of the Republic of South Africa, came from the Communists! When people start to label each other without reason, we should be on the alert. As soon as fanaticism has replaced reason, the church knows the powers have taken over.

Unfortunately, fanaticism can also occur on the "right side." An integrationist can be just as fanatical as a segregationist; he too can rob people of their freedom. In fact, sometimes we have to be more careful with the positive fanaticist than with the negative one.

One of the examples of positive fanaticism is Moral Re-Armament, a movement started by an American, Frank Buchman. It has had some influence in the church though little outside the church just before and after World War II.

M.R.A. wants a better world to come about through a chain of individual conversions that start at the level of the important people and, through their influence, reach the millions later. The real enemy, they say, is moral corruption; therefore, people must be morally rearmed and live according to the four absolutes: absolute love, absolute honesty, absolute purity, absolute selflessness. That sounds like quite a program! But be careful. As soon as the word "absolute" turns up, we are close to fanaticism.

The real mistake of this organization, which claims to have solved many national and international crises through personal conversions, is that the suprapersonal powers are not recognized. For M.R.A., society is nothing more than the sum of individuals involved; powers like the state, economy, money, sex, and mass media are only combinations of men. Any sociologist or politician knows how important persons are. He also knows that in our modern life each decision is influenced by both personal attitudes and larger, impersonal powers. Another mistake is the absoluteness of their demands. There are no absolutes on this earth. "Why do you call me good?" says Jesus. "Only my Father is good!" The absoluteness of their demands has made M.R.A. a fanatical group of people, who are often tempted to take refuge in distortions of the truth to persuade others to accept their point of view. A sad example of how even a good intention can of itself become an idol.

To Stand Still or Move Ahead

Finally, we recognize perverted powers in traditionalism and conservatism. (See Col. 3:9, 10.) Here we have to be very careful, because the words tradition and conservatism carry many meanings, and the debate about them soon tends to become emotional rather than rational. Paul says that the new nature is constantly renewed in the image of the Creator. Apparently the first great revolution, which makes the new nature possible, is not enough; constant renewal is required.

The need for renewal gives us a good yardstick with which to measure the powers: as soon as any power has set itself up as an idol and a god, it cannot tolerate renewal any more. Idols require blind obedience, not dialogue or personal relationships. Therefore, they always work with propaganda, labels, and generalizations. They insist that man should not change, that convictions are convictions, that, as Pilate said, what we have written we have written, and that being consistent is the most mature of all qualities of character.

These reactions are unbiblical and expressions of rebellion against God. Our God, in contrast to other gods, is an historical God: he is interested and active in the past, the present, and the future. He leads people toward tomorrow. He promises them a life in accordance with his will on this earth, and all our history moves toward this promised time.

The whole biblical story is one of movement, of change, and of renewal. Jesus is said to be the same yesterday, today, and always: He is a living person, who because of his unchanging love for man will always be finding ways to change people and renew them. Maturity in Christian terms, therefore, means flexibility and openness, the strength to change convictions, to apologize, to recant, to alter what one has written, to be inconsistent. The only conviction constant through all such change is *agape,* active love for our neighbors.

This obviously does not mean that Christianity stands

against tradition, or that Christianity is concentrating on changes rather than continuity. In effect, the Christian tradition is one of change, of continuous renewal. The New Testament reports the change of the old nature into the new; the early church shows an ongoing remolding of forms and structures of the church as well as of thought; the church fathers courageously put the message in the new language of the Greek culture. The Reformation boldly broke away from the traditional form of thinking and structure. In our own day the quiet but definite move toward unity among the denominations is an indication of the moving and changing character of the church.

Each generation has to face anew the double task of telling the old story in the language of the day and of being renewed structurally in the life of the church. If we compare the performances of any national church of today with the activities and fields of interest in churches fifty years ago, we see that the number of tasks has grown much larger. Being a church means being on the move. Some people think that the church is merely trying to be modern and attempts it with little success. They accuse the changing church of following the spirit of the time, of having fallen captive to this power. They believe in trusting the Lord to guard us rather than the sociological effectiveness or actuality of our church life.

Many churches do try desperately to be modern and "to meet the needs of modern people." This looks better than a conservative church that makes the past more important than the present. Yet renewal is more than keeping up with the times. Renewal means coming closer to the Christ and therefore closer to the people. Closeness in itself is no virtue.

The value of our presence is determined by our hope to bring Christ near to the people.

Conservatism and traditionalism are perverted powers: they bind people to yesterday and do not let them be open to new demands from the world which, after all, is not without God! The alternatives, however, are not progressivism and change. The biblical alternatives are called covenant and eschatology.

Covenant stands for the strange reality that God has made a pact with Israel and the church and has pledged to be faithful in the future as he has been faithful in the past. The tradition of Christianity is not the history of man's faithfulness to God; it is the account of God never leaving man. Therefore tradition is holy and must function in the church. Without tradition, the church would have to live with today and tomorrow only: that is unthinkable because we need the history of the love between God and man to know what to expect.

Tradition becomes traditionalism, and thus a perverted power, when it loses its historical character and becomes an eternal system. This system is not an attempt to grasp the truth in the language of the time and in the face of the challenge of the situation, but poses as truth itself. The covenant of God is always a living and mobile movement in which love is the only constant factor.

Eschatology, the other word for the biblical alternative to conservatism, is the term the church uses for its future. It speaks about the ultimate reality, like the return of the Messiah and the new universe. In the New Testament, one of the most important lines of proclamation is that the future has already begun. When God took on human form the final battle had started, and the final promise had begun to be realized. From now on, according to the New Testament, we write the last book of history.

Indeed, as the scientist has discovered, there is a terrific acceleration of history: inventions, population explosion, rapid social change. The Christian community sees this progress as evidence of the hand of the Lord, who is coming toward us, not out of the past but out of the future! We expect the new heaven and the new earth; we expect that God will make all things new; in that expectation we live and act.

The future has not only begun, it has also already been secured and revealed. It is no unknown territory: even when we do not know details, having only prophetic and visionary revelations about it, we know that the future is not a black hole in the ceiling of time but a mapped out road, with road service! Eschatological living, which could almost be called futuristic living, is the opposite of conservatism: it expects daily, in the words of the ecumenical patriarch, John R. Mott, great new things from God. Where things stand still, the church is suspicious; where they move, there is a mood of expectation and hope.

JUDGING THE POWERS

These are seven principles by which the church can start to judge the function of the powers of our day. When the powers isolate, bind, sow enmity, create loneliness, require idolatry, produce egotism or self-centeredness, conservatism and traditionalism, it is time to remember the invitation of the Messiah to join him in dethroning the powers. Where they help people to identify, liberate, reconcile, restore community, concentrate on Christ, serve, where they produce humility and a vivid awareness of God's covenant and future, we recognize the powers in their original service function.

Paul's Letter to the Colossians gives us a new insight into history. We see in all ages the struggle, and often the success, of the powers to become idols, to leave their service structure, and to dominate man. Throughout the Old Testament we are told about this struggle inside and outside Israel. When Christ came the struggle was brought into the open and the first decisive victory over the powers was won.

In Europe, during the last war, D-day was the moment when the allied troops fought their way back into the continent. The war did not end then, but all people, including the enemy, knew that the final victory was only a question of time.

So, in Christ, D-day came: the powers were exposed with their real faces, and they were fatally overpowered. Since then we see them tumble. First they lose their grip on the church, although they keep trying to get back at the helm! Then we see them fall in the world. Continent after continent starts to rebel against the control of the perverted powers. Religions of all sorts, Christianity included, tremble.

Often it is the proclamation of the Christian gospel that starts a liberation movement from the idols. Many times the church recognizes God's work in the world in secular movements. Perhaps the most moving example is the Christian mission in Africa. When the gospel was preached in Africa, when hospitals were built, and when Christianity was shown in daily life in that tremendous continent, the powers were forced to leave their position of control. The old idols in the trees and the phenomena of nature—rain, hail, thunder—

stopped having control, man became man, and a new adventure of freedom started.

Of course the powers do not commit suicide; they have to be captured and dethroned, and they often escape again. Nazism was such a new attempt by the powers to gain control over many again; McCarthyism was another; communism in its dogmatic form is a third. All three, and many more, although quite different from one another, started terrific battles to recapture the freedom of man. Two of them were overpowered, although not totally, and the third is in inner conflict. Communism, in most instances, is still a perverted power, although not a static one, and the church holds its breath to see the new developments. So we learn to see history as the stage of the mission of Christ and his people for struggling with the powers, exposing them and checking them. We as a Christian community will be called to overpower the perverted powers of our day—not by using means of force and brutality, but the ones Paul describes.

In the final chapter, we will try to answer the most difficult questions of all. How do we effectively take part in this fight? Are we only called to defend ourselves against the perverted powers, or are we also charged to attack them, convert them, and make them servants again? Is this a challenge to the church alone, or also to those who do not believe that Jesus is the Messiah? Do we, as a younger generation, have a special task?

CHAPTER FOUR

Power Struggle

How do we participate in Christ's mission toward the world, especially in relation to the powers? I repeat two remarks made earlier: the real discussion about our part in Christ's mission has to take place where we are living and working. We shall therefore have to leave open the most important questions in this chapter. Secondly, on paper there are no answers. Maybe in life we can find solutions. Maybe we have to be content to see the questions and avoid the wrong answers. A good question is obviously better than a bad answer or an answer to a question that nobody asked! In any case, we are not short of questions!

OUR CHOICE AS CHRISTIANS

The first question is: what kind of position do we take in life? Do we make choices, or do we let life come as it is? Do we submit to the powers, or do we struggle with them? When we look around us we see that there are three basic positions: we can worship the powers, we can quietly submit ourselves to them, or we can struggle with them. Worshiping the powers means that we willingly let ourselves be enslaved by them. We become fanatics and traditionalists, we fight for ourselves and our little concerns, we couldn't care less about the others. Submitting to the powers means that we try to ignore them and live a quiet life. We do not mingle in politics or take a position on any issues. We are sympathetic listeners to all parties, but never commit ourselves; we have to think of ourselves too, we say, and of our future and family. Struggling with the powers means that we join the minority that takes sides; we enter the discussion and the struggle. In less theological terms, do we unquestioningly commit ourselves to our society, presuming it is always right, do we simply vegetate in it, or do we participate critically?

This choice has to be made rather early in our life, because it is almost like choosing a vocation. To choose critical participation, which means both loyalty and detachment, means to choose a party. Those who struggle with the powers are found everywhere, in all parts of the church. They are not bound by a denomination: they form a unity that transcends all party politics. Their unity is stable, built on truth. Belonging to this group requires study and reading and continually being on guard. It means acceptance of a position as a watchdog and taking that position for life.

I learned the term critical participation in the first Ecumenical Youth Assembly in Europe at Lausanne in 1960. Seventeen hundred people came to this assembly, almost equally representing Europe and the rest of the world. Without having planned it, all the speakers called our attention to the same situation: Europe itself and the church in Europe were in a precarious position and it would not do to pretend that all was well. But, they all said, this was our continent and our community; therefore, we had better not back out but stick with it and do something about it. "Otherwise," said one of the speakers during a session with a discussion group, "I would rather see you leave. We have nothing to say to those who want to use us without committing themselves to the task ahead of us, nor do we have anything to say to those who want to eat from our table without paying. What we need are people who keep their eyes open to the real situation, who are willing to be constructive and to engage in the ungrateful task of criticism."

We discovered similar conditions in the church. We all criticized it freely: it is not attractive, it is dull, it is a ghetto, the church speaks jargon that no one understands, it sings hymns that are neither theologically nor aesthetically acceptable, it uses copies of historical buildings rather than places for meeting and worship belonging to our own time, it is socially and politically conservative, and it is too often a one-man show. Nevertheless, we belong to it. Our criticism stems more from a form of hurt love than from a wholly negative feeling. Therefore we do not think of leaving it or of just sitting in it as angry but silent young men; we want to be part of the power to renew it. Out of these considerations grew the certainty that to be a man means to be a critical participant in our communities.

The question now is: do we want to be critical participants? Perhaps the better question is: can we carry out this commitment? Are we able to bear the tension that it creates in our lives? Are we strong enough to take the responsibilities? Many sociologists have said in the last ten years that this mature, and therefore critical, participation is beyond the ability of a younger generation. They say society is too complex and youth too confused. Only those who come from the best families, which were always the critical and construc-

said one of the speakers during a session with a discussion group, "I would rather see you leave. We have nothing to say to those who want to use us without committing themselves to the task ahead of us, nor do we have anything to say to those who want to eat from our table without paying. What we need are people who keep their eyes open to the real situation, who are willing to be constructive and to engage in the ungrateful task of criticism."

We discovered similar conditions in the church. We all criticized it freely: it is not attractive, it is dull, it is a ghetto, the church speaks jargon that no one understands, it sings hymns that are neither theologically nor aesthetically acceptable, it uses copies of historical buildings rather than places for meeting and worship belonging to our own time, it is socially and politically conservative, and it is too often a one-man show. Nevertheless, we belong to it. Our criticism stems more from a form of hurt love than from a wholly negative feeling. Therefore we do not think of leaving it or of just sitting in it as angry but silent young men; we want to be part of the power to renew it. Out of these considerations grew the certainty that to be a man means to be a critical participant in our communities.

The question now is: do we want to be critical participants? Perhaps the better question is: can we carry out this commitment? Are we able to bear the tension that it creates in our lives? Are we strong enough to take the responsibilities? Many sociologists have said in the last ten years that this mature, and therefore critical, participation is beyond the ability of a younger generation. They say society is too complex and youth too confused. Only those who come from the best families, which were always the critical and construc-

care less about the others. Submitting to the powers means that we try to ignore them and live a quiet life. We do not mingle in politics or take a position on any issues. We are sympathetic listeners to all parties, but never commit ourselves; we have to think of ourselves too, we say, and of our future and family. Struggling with the powers means that we join the minority that takes sides; we enter the discussion and the struggle. In less theological terms, do we unquestioningly commit ourselves to our society, presuming it is always right, do we simply vegetate in it, or do we participate critically?

This choice has to be made rather early in our life, because it is almost like choosing a vocation. To choose critical participation, which means both loyalty and detachment, means to choose a party. Those who struggle with the powers are found everywhere, in all parts of the church. They are not bound by a denomination: they form a unity that transcends all party politics. Their unity is stable, built on truth. Belonging to this group requires study and reading and continually being on guard. It means acceptance of a position as a watchdog and taking that position for life.

I learned the term critical participation in the first Ecumenical Youth Assembly in Europe at Lausanne in 1960. Seventeen hundred people came to this assembly, almost equally representing Europe and the rest of the world. Without having planned it, all the speakers called our attention to the same situation: Europe itself and the church in Europe were in a precarious position and it would not do to pretend that all was well. But, they all said, this was our continent and our community; therefore, we had better not back out but stick with it and do something about it. "Otherwise,"

that they lose their divine character and exist simply as forces to serve us.

When we expose the powers, we expose them as defeated on the cross, and we give thanks. In other words: the victory has been won. We are only cleaning up; the outcome was decided a long time ago. We give thanks; and the way we give thanks is to be included in the process of subduing the powers under the feet of Christ.

The last question to be put is: How?

Affirming Faith in Christ

How, for instance, do we show that we do not believe in the powers? We need to demonstrate our rejection of powers, since so many people do believe in them. It is also necessary for ourselves because, like the Colossians, we need to be reminded of our own faith in Christ alone. When, in Nazi Germany, Hitler demanded that the church worship his theories and actions, a remnant of the German churches refused. Together they wrote the Barmen Declaration. Its first article reads:

Jesus Christ, as He testified to us in Holy Scripture, is the one Word of God which we have to hear and which we have to trust and obey in life and death. We reject the false doctrine that the Church can and should recognize other events and powers, figures and truths as revelations of God.

This statement was of course directed against such myths as Nordic blood, the Aryan race, and the God-sent führer, Adolf Hitler. It set forth nothing new but did provide a firm reminder that the church has but one Lord.

It is significant that in our liturgies there is no mention of the powers when we state our beliefs. Every Sunday, or whenever a congregation of Christ gathers, we are reminded that we do not believe in the powers. The church gets nervous, and rightly so, when people start to "believe" in other powers. We are reminded of ugly historical realities when politicians affirm their belief in "our free country" or "the right of each individual to live as he thinks good." These principles may represent high values, but they are not the content of the Christian faith. Therefore, they will have to be exposed when they request the belief of other people as well. The shortcomings of these beliefs are always shown in history, and the church often has only to remind us of a few historical facts to have us realize that we had better reserve one firm and central belief as a model on which to base our lives.

Of course, all people are free to believe what they think is right and, at least in our Western society, almost everybody can propagandize for what he believes. This freedom is not without limits; certain people with moral beliefs or political ideas that are unacceptable to the community, advocates of homosexuality, for instance, or the Communists in some countries, are not allowed to conduct propaganda campaigns for their ideas. The Christian church, which knows that freedom belongs to the essence of the gospel, should always fight for the people's right to have a free press and freedom to propagate ideas, even when she herself holds their ideas to be false.

The Christian community knows that propaganda of truth enslaves as much as the propaganda of lies. A passion for freedom in which people can decide on the basis of the fullest evidence possible includes the risk of letting people campaign with the wrong arguments. The church should refute or ignore false and ridiculous ideas rather than campaign to have them suppressed.

Only in cases where free propaganda of ideas would endanger the health of society and would render the protection from sickness and madness ineffective, may the church reluctantly and with great care speak against the freedom to propagandize. But whenever ideas start to enslave people or to claim their worship, she must relentlessly expose them; she must speak and write against the false claims of the powers.

Let us look at the race issue again. Here is a power that has held people in bondage and has made it impossible for millions to be as free as other persons in the same community. The church must proclaim that Christ on the cross has disarmed the powers, including that of race. The church knows that faith in Christ includes the basic equality of all people, and therefore the basic equality of their rights. The task of the church is to make a public spectacle of the race power by living its defeat.

Wherever a Christian community is integrated, the power of race is seen to be overpowered. People can see that all their fears and prejudices have no logical grounds. The exposure of the powers is like charming snakes or taming lions. These activities show that the power of snake and lion are not ultimate. The church has the means and strength, through God, to charm and tame the powers. It does so by simply not obeying them.

I am told that in Germany funerals are becoming more and more expensive. People may be in debt for years to pay off the last expression of respect to the dead. One day a very well-to-do man died. When his last will was opened, it said that he wanted to be buried as he was born, poor and helpless. He requested that, at his inexpensive funeral, a letter of his own should be read, in which he, with considerable humor, attacked this new power in life. Such exposures of the powers are strong and effective.

Humor and imagination are strong weapons against the powers, which are always dead serious. A sharp cartoon that can help people ridicule a power often does more good than a whole series of sermons on the subject. The moment a Christian community or even an individual member of it cannot laugh heartily at a power, that power has enslaved him and is his master.

In a culture that more and more conforms to the same pressures and adopts the same attitudes, examples of individuality are basic examples of freedom. We have the Christian community in which to train ourselves in these exercises for freedom. This is no plea for nonconformity. Freedom and nonconformity have in common the fact that they do not imitate, but nonconformity is a new prison: the prison of the pressure of constantly having to be different. Freedom is functional: it is exercised not only for oneself, but also for others.

In East Germany a young pastor was sent to a new pastorate in a small town where the Communists were very anti-church. Upon his arrival, both he and all his furniture were searched for "capitalist propaganda materials"; it took days before he got all his papers and permits. The first weeks in his new place were quite uncomfortable. He was telephoned during the night and laughed at in the streets. His license was checked many times, and his wife was harassed in the shops.

After some time the local boss of the party fell out of grace with the authorities and was sent away as secretary to a cooperative farm near the Polish border. And the pastor? On holidays, he looked up his former enemy and went fishing with him for a few days. "I have enough friends," he said. "He hasn't."

Do you get the point of the story? There was a power that got out of hand, sowed enmity, and indeed put itself between people. But the pastor exposed it and cut it down to size. Between the pastor and the political leader there were great differences of belief and conviction; but that is not necessarily bad. That this difference created hate and enmity, however, was the sign that the power had become rebellious. The Communist remained a Communist, and the minister a Christian, but the power between them had lost its divine overtones. The minister had shown that he was a free man but not necessarily a nonconformist.

Exposing the Powers

Making a public spectacle out of the powers can be done in a number of ways. A youth group in the Netherlands sent a letter to the editor of a national newspaper, exposing some of the fanatical attempts to keep Indonesia as a Dutch colony back in 1947. There was a national outcry against them, but the discussion had begun. Youth groups have to learn to recognize powers around them and simply denounce them. The effects are often remarkable.

We only have to show the courage not to believe in the powers. Hans Christian Anderson wrote the story about the emperor's new clothes. The tailors had said that only capable people could see the new clothes, so no one dared to express the fact that he did not see a thing for fear of being recognized as an incapable person. Everybody was silent—until a child cried: "But he has nothing on at all."

Our role is that of the child. When all people are silent we cry: "But he has nothing on at all!" Then others will take courage and wake up as well.

In the Bible the Christians are often called "the first fruits of the new creation." We are the first swallows that announce the summer to all. We are the starters, and others will carry on the fight. The role of the "unmaskers" is not popular. The first people who unmasked fascism or McCarthyism had a difficult time. The first people to recognize the rebellion of the power of race in South Africa and the United States were relentlessly persecuted, but the powers they attacked were exposed; their hour had come, and they knew it.

One of the tasks of the Christian church is to tell the story of the powers overpowered: those Jesus exposed on the cross, and those now exposed in the world. We must learn how to publish and spread these stories, to hand them from reader to reader. As Paul says, "This letter should also be read in the Church of Laodicea."

We also have to learn to dethrone the power of propaganda, and make it what it originally was—the servant of information. We can do that in several ways. First we can check out the situation for ourselves. Personal contacts are the best attacks on impersonal powers. Certainly, as people who belong to a universal community, we should make much more of the effect of our personal influence on the impersonal powers.

The greatest task for us in this respect may well be the relationship between the Western world and the Communist world. The church exists in both, and there is a lively discussion going on as to what the role of the church should be, both in a Communist country and in the relation between Western and Eastern people. Our thesis is that propaganda is a questionable tool in that discussion. Since propaganda tells only negative stories about the other party, it can hardly help people to understand the real issues of the discussion between the two political systems.

Let nobody think there are no differences between Eastern and Western societies! Between the so-called bourgeois democracies of the West and the so-called socialist democracies of the East there is a considerable difference in outlook and in practice. The differences, however, are not those of hell and paradise. Any Western Christian who says that behind the iron curtain hell's territory begins is an atheist at heart. The Christian church has always believed, and still professes, that Christ is Lord over all the earth. This includes the East. Communist territory too is, in the words of Pastor Johannes Hamel from East Germany, God's beloved world! We Christians therefore have nothing to fear and all to gain in our contacts with those who do not believe in Christ and who reject his church.

Propaganda selects the news and so distorts the truth. It shows contempt for people's ability to make up their own minds and is an expression of fear of the real situation. Propaganda can be exposed in a number of ways. In the West, at least, one can easily read the other side of the story, either in direct sources written from the other side or through the more or less objective reporting of people who have been in the other camp.

The last way is the most effective. It seems obvious to

me that young Christians must take the earliest possible opportunity of traveling, for instance, in Eastern Europe or other socialist countries. Those journeys should be prepared carefully and guided responsibly. The church should inform the government of the home country, which is often extremely concerned about these journeys because they have become used to thinking in terms of isolation and attack. The travelers must also tell the government of the country to be visited that they are coming and explain the objectives of the trip. Most important, the guides in the other country should be our Christian brethren there.

Many young Western European Christians have traveled in Eastern Europe and discussed issues with people there. Very few, if any, have become Communists, but all of them have got another perspective on what communism really is, really wants, and really does to the Christian church. Most important, the power of propaganda has been overpowered, and people have felt free to make their own decisions based on facts.

Most of our anti-Communist convictions stem from propaganda. We have heard so many horror stories about the Communists, and the Communists have heard so many horror stories about us, that we each believe the other to be a deplorable and cruel criminal. When we meet, we discover normal people who differ essentially on principle and practical questions, but we can start a conversation with them. We can listen, talk, and convince. We need communication to keep the other side in perspective and to help us remember that our political opponents are human beings rather than mere ideas or principles with which we disagree.

At a student conference in Europe a few years ago, a Communist came to address the Christian participants. The conference was enthusiastic, not because the address was so brilliant, but because the Communist was obviously an ordinary man and a believer (in his own ideology!) as well. To refuse to see Communists as real people considerably weakens our position in the debate! Only when we recognize that the partner in the discussion is a human being and reacts, thinks, eats, sleeps, and laughs as we all do, are we ready for the real discussion.

In such relationships we need to concentrate on the people in Communist or Marxist countries such as Eastern Europe and Cuba as well as the people of the developing countries. With all our mass media and channels of news, we are still able to shut out the hunger- and poverty-stricken areas of the world from our minds. We can discover many of our faults in personal encounters and exchange programs; visits with people from other countries are essential for our struggle with the powers. Since we are among the rich nations, the poorer countries will have to tell us some unpleasant stories. We soothe our consciences by parading our programs of foreign aid. Yet we earn more in the developing countries by paying low prices for raw materials than we give in aid.

This is propaganda to tell one figure and hide the other, giving an incomplete account. Christians are called to know all the figures and to make a public spectacle of them in order to prepare our countries for serious consideration of the issues. We must remember that in a democracy, a government can do little when public opinion has not been prepared for action. A community of Christians, be it large or small, can be the conscience of the nation and prepare the way for political action.

All our Christian giving is helpful and biblically legitimate only when it takes place in the context of the whole world situation. To take up an offering in a church and send a million dollars or pounds or guilders to a developing country from which we buy basic raw materials at a fantastically low price is hypocrisy as long as we do not expose the real powers that are at stake. During the last ten years the rich countries gave about 47½ billion dollars to the poor countries. Since most of this money came in loans, the developing countries have to pay interest which amounts to 21 billion dollars. In that same time the prices of raw material and agricultural goods were lowered, and the income of the developing countries decreased by about 13 billion dollars. The actual amount of foreign aid, therefore, was not more than 13½ billion dollars. If we assume that one third of the world's population is aiding two thirds, the total foreign aid adds up to something less than one dollar in ten years for each person receiving aid! This shows what happens when the power of wealth gets out of hand.

I am not implying that foreign aid is bad or that the price of raw materials on the world market is the only determining factor in the fight against hunger and poverty. I am simply saying that foreign aid becomes hypocrisy when it is portrayed as *the* effective means of combatting poverty and hunger. It is important for us to listen to the people in the developing countries who are telling us why and how we could change things.

To make a public spectacle of the powers requires study. Fact finding and basic research are essential elements in the struggle with generalization and myths. Basic research is not difficult in an age of libraries and universities. One local council of churches, one local congregation, or even one youth group, yes, even a small part of a youth group, can play a significant role in the publication of the facts of the issue under discussion. An ecumenical youth group in England once made a survey of the social conditions in their town, then confronted the city council. The city fathers were first annoyed and then happy with such "critical participation," and they promised to take action. The press reported the whole affair adequately, and the conscience of the city was awakened. Above all, the powers were weakened.

A small church in Africa once assembled materials on the social ills of growing urbanization in the country. The young people simply took all that was known and published it in certain local and national newspapers. The result was that the opposition in Parliament took up the case, probably for political reasons. The government sighed and took action. A power was checked.

The Church and the Powers

The life of the Christian church in relation to the powers is critical. We are the proud descendants of the prophets of Israel, who taught the people of God that service to Jahveh was intimately related with service to the poor and the destitute. We are the proud friends of Jesus of Nazareth, who during all three years of his public ministry struggled gloriously with the powers. Both the prophets and Christ himself encountered severe reactions from the powers. The prophets were even killed, and so was Christ. It looked as if the powers had so much strength that they could even crucify the Lord of Glory. God had been edged out of his own creation, and the powers ruled it. Then, at the cross, the roles were reversed. The powers had to come out of hiding and show their antagonism to God. When Jesus was raised from the dead, the situation had completely changed: the powers were overpowered.

From that moment on there has been no reason to despair about the outcome. A fight with the powers has resulted in their downfall. Nevertheless, people have to go the way of the cross to come to victory. We should never portray the power struggle as a quick way to success; it is a sure way, but a hazardous one. We see the risks in the race struggle, the wealth struggle, the struggle over money, politics, or sex. It is a road only for strong people: those who are strengthened by the Lord and by each other.

The first stage on the way is that of making a public spectacle of the powers. First by living the victory over the powers: by showing that they can be checked. The man who does not drink because he is driving and the people who defeat the power of hate by showing love for their enemies are doing the same thing. Careful study of the issues at stake, traveling to meet people who think and behave differently, a prudent use of our Christian brethren in other countries are all very helpful roads to come to a mastering of the powers of our time. The most powerful weapon of the rebellious powers is to cover up the truth, and therefore the most important action is to uncover their machinations.

Sex

Look at the power of sex. The great silence and the reluctance of people to talk openly about sexual questions has held generations under a spell. It has made the power of sex mightier and mightier. In our generation we reap the bitter harvest of that silence, because we seem to have to make up for it! An allusion to sex is enough to make people prick up their ears; sex in an advertisement is a sure means of attracting customers. We can sum it up in two words: sex reigns. What really suffers from the fear of sex is sex itself. It has a hard time finding its proper service function and remains on the throne either of our open admiration or of our fear.

What is needed is clear: we want sex to serve us, not to dominate our lives. We want it normally, without its rebellious forms of either pornography or perversions. In order to restore sex to its natural proportions, we will first of all have to learn the truth about it. We need open talk about it in the family and in the school. If possible, sex education should be carried on in mixed groups; and, even more important, there should be married people present. So long as we have grown up physically and are not yet married, sex will always be trying to dominate us. Only when we learn to see it in the context of the whole of life, rather than in the limited scope of the time when it is largely forbidden territory, shall we be able to master it. The openness may well have to come from the children rather than from parents and teachers. The questions of teen-agers and unmarried young adults can serve the purpose of bringing the discussion into the open.

In a time when ideas seem less meaningful than hard facts, life tends to be ruled by what we can touch. Our bodies are the most, if not the only, certain possessions we have. This consciousness of our bodies is reflected in our sexual tensions. The influence of society is also present; the more impersonal our relationships are in the world, the more we build up a necessity for intimate relationships. More intimate relationships than those in which our skin plays a role do not exist.

Our approach to and our use of the sexual powers must be totally rethought. Casual repetitions of outdated values do not help. Daring experiments in which we hope to discover new values have not helped much either. The only way left is a probing and honest dialogue between those who are in conflict about sex and those who have succeeded in making sex a servant in their lives. The church has never been good at that dialogue. Sex makes us nervous; we quickly fall back on quoting Bible texts out of context to each other. This is no more helpful than the silence we had before.

We have taken quite a step when we can honestly tell each other that we all, youth and adults, have trouble in keeping this giant of a power in its place. From there we may be able, again, to start avoiding the wrong answers and approaches; we may even find a few answers. But nobody should think that it is impossible to live with a conversation without answers. On the contrary, life may be richer when a constant dialogue goes on to discover answers than when the answers have all been found. Regardless of the probability of finding a solution, there is a basic need for a dialogue, a fearless one, and soon.

Once we face the sexual question, we will have to discover a new discipline—not an individual one, but a common one. That discipline should start by renouncing the power of conformity in these matters. If young people indulge in sexual experimentation only because everybody else does it, they show themselves to be conformists.

It would be dangerous, however, to accuse young people

of conformity and leave it at that. They are not asking for a judgment but are in need of clarification: Why has the old morality broken down? Has society changed? Then, what is proper behavior in this new society? Is the new sexual experimentation an expression of physical need, as it appears to be? Or does it arise from a deeper need, involving the body and the spirit, the relation to persons as well as the relation to the whole of society?

We have already seen that judgment and critique did not stop the developments in people's sexual behavior: We only succeeded in giving a minority a bad conscience. But we don't need that. We need a new discipline, one not taken for granted but worked out together and provisionally accepted. Until the open dialogue starts, however, a discipline will be one guided by fear, and that is not up to our standards. Let us first make a public spectacle of our fears and lack of confidence.

Politics

The power of politics is also a formidable one. Occasionally it gets out of control and becomes a confusing enslaving force rather than a servant structure. A beautiful example of uncontrolled power may be found in the primaries for the American presidential election. Not only for the outsider but also for many Americans, this has become a despicable struggle for power. The really important political issues are driven into the background more and more, and what is left is a fight for power between interest groups. The major American newspapers have almost given up trying to get the fight back on the level of the issues; the election machines of the candidates are the only powers speaking.

The people of the United States are enslaved in a lack of knowledge. To vote for any candidate has become an emotional outlet, not an objective decision on politics. For the outsider looking critically at American politics, the rebellious powers reign: there is no discussion, but enmity; people are not free to choose, but are taken up in an unreal fight between candidates; there is fanaticism rather than renewal. The powers reign.

What a blessing it would be if the churches could step in and make a public spectacle out of the powers! This is no plea for the church to "enter politics." Nevertheless, a voice in the middle of life should interpret to the people the real issues behind the candidates. This voice would force the candidates to speak seriously about politics rather than making derogatory remarks about their opponents.

The primaries may be beyond the influence of local voices. The job should start in smaller communities with the churches taking an active part in local politics, not as a power but as an educational instrument. Before we commit ourselves politically we have to understand what politics are and what the issues are. If we do not do that, we make the political debate an open arena for the emotions and teach people to vote for the man who promises most, for the man who has the nicest, most confidence-inspiring face. Whoever makes such superficial characteristics the basis of his vote should go back to school and study history.

USING THE POWERS

So the powers must be exposed when they have become perverted or rebellious. They must also be discarded as garments. Let us take that literally. Paul says: "Jesus did not use them any longer to cover him. He laid them aside." Now that is interesting. Most people who are willing to expose the rebellious powers would continue to use them in their perverted form. But here the gospel says No! The created powers are our servants, but their perverted form we do not touch. Paul gives a whole list of them: perverted sex (lust), perverted worship (idolatry), perverted indignation (anger), perverted interest (passion), perverted difference of opinion (malice), perverted language (cursing, filthy talk), perverted truth (lie), perverted diversity (division of race and culture). (See Col. 3:5-11.)

The church has always had difficulty in making the simple distinction between the powers and their perversions. It usually recognized the rebellious powers but had a hard time in recognizing that, without perversion, the powers were a created reality with a positive task even today. During the history of the Christian church we see over and over again that certain groups realize the rebellion of the powers and refuse to use them at all. Politics is a dirty game, they say, and they refuse to be involved. They do not see that although politics is easily corrupted into a dirty game, the power itself is necessary for life together. The vocation of the politician is an essential one: he is called to keep society in order and, with the help of the servant powers, to make the world a better place to live in.

"Education is dangerous for Christians because it teaches our children to doubt and to be dissatisfied with the life they have." How right this remark, which I once heard, is! Many families have been disrupted because of the difference in the educational backgrounds of parents and children. In the last two centuries education has also been misused for propaganda purposes. About eighty years ago many teachers in Europe were avowed atheists and regarded it their duty to liberate school children from their religious superstitions.

In Communist countries, education is equivalent to Marxist indoctrination. We are guilty of indoctrination in the West, too. Compare two history textbooks: one used in Roman Catholic schools, and one used in nonsectarian schools. They are like accounts of two different worlds! Such faults in our educational system should never bring a Christian to be an anti-educationist. They should make him, as a student, as a citizen, and as a future parent, a champion of better education.

This power of education can also be brought back to its original function of service. We shall not use the perverted power, however. We refuse to use education for purposes of indoctrination. We will not use the perverted power of mammon (rebellious money) to buy influence and power; we will not use the perverted forms of sex; we will not use the perverted power of the nation—and our refusal will be for positive reasons. We do not abstain from the use of the perverted powers out of fear of being contaminated by them or because "there are certain things Christians don't do!" but simply because we have learned the right use of the powers.

It is important to learn the correct use of the powers; the victory in itself is not enough. The victor must now take over the power of the victim. Christ himself, since the battle was fought and won in his name, now has to dictate to the conquered power what its future shall be. The victory over the power does not mean that from now on we live in anarchy: that the power is dead and no other power has taken over. That would mean chaos, and it often does. Think once again over the practical examples of sex, money, nationalism, grades, and propaganda. In each case, when the rebellious power has been exposed, only half the job has been done. Now the new organization of roles has to be thought out and implemented.

When Germany surrendered and the power of Nazism was conquered, a new Germany had to be built up. We had to choose between many alternatives in dealing with this conquered power. What did we choose? Revenge, forgiveness, or restitution? Should we unite or divide the allied sectors of the country? Whom should we ask to lead the country into its new life? The Germans themselves and the leaders they chose, or the men we trusted? What happens in the stage immediately after the defeat of the rebellious power is very important.

At this stage, the Apostle gives us the clue of indeed binding the powers to Jesus' chariot. In concrete language that simply means that the church does not only expose and fight the rebellious powers, it also develops the new function of the powers as servants. The church, said Bonhoeffer, is Christ existing as community. In this self-evaluation of the church it accepts responsibility for the situation after the fight. The powers are recognized in their service capacity and are assigned to their respective duties.

When Paul speaks about "putting to death" anger and passion and greed, is he not speaking about something rather violent? Is not violence in itself a perverted power? Let us look at World War II again. In it, evil was eradicated by violence. That violence was undoubtedly necessary, and it hastened the end of the war. But did it free people? Did it bring the Nazis to conversion and reconciliation with other people, or did it only subdue them?

Here we have to look at the third phrase Paul uses to describe Christ's struggle with the powers: he led them in his triumphal procession. For a moment we see Rome: tens of thousands of people shouting in admiration for the great soldiers coming home. Behind the chariot of the commander are the captives, a public spectacle, bound to the chariot of their conqueror. We should be attentive to that last point: The powers are bound to Jesus' chariot. In other words, it is not enough to make a spectacle out of them; we also have to keep them close to the real victor.

Perhaps somebody is already questioning what he has read thus far. Is it really necessary to bring the whole New Testament into an argument that is a normal part of everybody's life? What is so specifically Christian about making a public spectacle out of the powers? If we look around us, it is perfectly clear that it is mostly the non-Christians who are really struggling with the powers, while the churches are worshiping them!

In the history of Europe the socialists and the atheists have a better record of fighting the powers than the Christians. During the war years, the Communists who fought in the resistance movements were often better fighters against evil than many of us. Why do theologians have to insist that only the church can be engaged in the power struggle? Why do we have to give Christians credit for what they often do not do?

These are serious questions, and they deserve our attention. First, we are happy to say that indeed many non-Christians are engaged in the power struggle. The church commits a sin by making a problem out of the non-Christian battle against the powers. Whenever people who do not recognize Jesus as the Messiah team up with him and his friends, we rejoice. " 'Many . . . will come from east and west [says Jesus] to feast with Abraham, Isaac, and Jacob in the kingdom of Heaven.' " (Matt. 8:11, NEB)

The non-Christian, engaged in the power struggle, is no problem. We expect him there. Is Jesus not Lord of all things and all people? Should he not be expected to work in the hearts and minds of those who have not yet accepted him as their master? The mission of God goes through Christ to all men. The fields which Jesus sees are white for the harvest: Christ sees fruit in many more people around him than we sometimes care to acknowledge. So let us rejoice in the Christian church about humanists and atheists, about nonbelievers and pagans, who join the struggle against the rebellious powers. But mark! It is not enough to cast off the evil—we have to put on new clothes, says Paul. To be engaged in the struggle with the perverted "authorities and thrones" is one thing, but it is not enough.

I once had an enlightening discussion with some Latin American students. We were talking about the coming revolution in their lands. Latin America is a magnificent continent, but the order of most of the societies is open to serious question. A few share all wealth, while the masses are hungry and illiterate. Often the poor are even used as slaves by the clique that happens to possess the means. It is clear that this will have to change. A large group of intellectuals, and especially students, now feel that nothing less than a revolution can change the system under which they live.

The place of the Christian student in these revolutionary

patterns was being discussed. Most of the students were certain that Christian participation in the revolution was necessary. Then a Roman Catholic girl made a penetrating remark. "When the revolution succeeds," she said, "only half the job is done. Because afterwards we shall have to learn compassion and forgiveness for those we have had to push down from their powerful seats!"

Compassion is very important. We, in postwar Europe, have done little in that direction. We smote the idols, but we did not clothe ourselves in the proper garments of compassion, gentleness, humility, and patience. We often turned our victory into a rebellious power, and so the story started all over again. Control over the powers is exercised just as Paul has taught us in his letter to the Ephesians. Jomo Kenyatta in Kenya, who was once the feared leader of the Mau-Mau in his country, has understood this better than many Christians. When he had won a bitter victory over the power of colonialism, he started a program of reconciliation and forgiveness that not only restored many people to confidence but also gave order to his land.

In order to control the powers, we need great strength. Christians do not expect that strength from themselves: we look to our Lord for guidance.

Christian worship is, in principle, a good example of our search for God's help. We already saw that the worship of the Christian church is conceived to express belief in Christ rather than the powers. In the sermon—ideally at least— the rebellious powers are named and their perversion is demonstrated. When we take up the offering, we attack the power of money: we profess that we get our possessions from the hands of God and that we have to use them, not to worship them. The offering is, therefore, an important part of the worship service. In the intercessory prayers we remind ourselves of God's ongoing love for other people and of the fact that we are called to be instrumental in telling them about his love for them. We also confess that Christ is the one who helps us and not the powers, which are only tools in his hands.

The sacraments play an important part. Baptism is the sign and seal that we died with Christ and that the powers have no ultimate power over us: they cannot separate us from the love of Christ. In baptism also we are raised with Christ and are clad with the new garments of the new creation. In the Eucharist we are again made part of the death and resurrection of the Lord, and we "proclaim his death until he comes." As often as we take part in this communion, we realize that the center of our existence lies with the Messiah rather than with "the weak powers of the world." Of course, many of those things are not clear in our worship services. Therefore, we are called to participate critically, that is, to renew our worship so that these elements become visible and a source of strength for our participation in the mission of Christ.

A UNITED STAND

It has become clear, I hope, that a younger generation in the church is a critical part of the struggle with the powers. One item may still need a few extra remarks. We said earlier that the rebellious powers always try to divide. Not only do they try to separate us from the love of God, but they have also built a wall of separation between Jews and pagans. (See Rom. 8 and Eph. 2:14.) Christ broke that wall down, and he ripped apart the iron curtain we had built up between God and ourselves. The Christian church is called to join God in Christ's work of destruction. Its work toward unity is a struggle with powers that is central to our living with the gospel. Unity is not only an essential mark of the church, but also an essential element of life itself. Let us look at our involvement, as younger people in the church, in the unity between the churches, the unity between the generations, and the unity of church and world.

The unity of the church has always spoken to the imagination of a younger generation. The simple reason for this is the experience of belonging together, not only as contemporaries but also as people who are engaged in the same struggle to make the Christian faith a living reality in the world. Sometimes the churches fail to see that their younger laity (who, by the way, are full members of the same body) have a hard time coming to grips with the Christian life. Youth feel themselves called to master life in the society in which they are placed, and that calls for full participation in its activities.

Adolescence is an adventure that requires all one's energy. During this period the gospel becomes something different from the stories we have heard in church school. Jesus becomes a strong, demanding personality rather than simply the friendly, comforting man he was before. It becomes clear that belonging to Christ means belonging to a new people with a new outlook on life.

This is challenging and exciting at the same time. It requires again all available energy. The crippling division between the churches is unbearable, and even unreal, during this time. The important discoveries, usually made in camps

and conferences, are made together with young Christians of
other denominations. It is a matter of course to discover the
unity of the church. But this discovery of unity is quickly
perverted by the conflicting and competitive existence of the
denominations. A large group of younger churchmen escape
from the dangerous position of unity into a complacent and
sometimes even fanatical adherence to the different confes-
sions. Isolation becomes bearable, and we do not even want
to meet the others any more. In the Christian community,
"apartheid" reigns between Roman and Orthodox, Angli-
can and Protestant members of the church.

The situation is changing, however. Within the church
there is a minority that sees that the powers of individuality
have run away from their function. Often a minority of
young people have been leading the church as a whole. The
word minority needs stressing. It is nonsense to say that
young people are for unity, while the adults waver. Today
young people are often more conservative than the older
ones. But there are renewers in both groups, and within the
saving remnant the younger ones are often leading.

How? In all sorts of ways. In the Netherlands not long
ago, young people of the Roman and Protestant churches or-
ganized a one-day congress with five thousand young Christians under the theme "Five Loaves and Three Fishes." The
topic was taken from the New Testament story of the feed-
ing of the five thousand, and the choice of the theme expressed both their dependence upon the work of Christ and
their unity. They decided that all over the Netherlands local
groups would start to bring together Protestants and Roman
Catholics to see together what the Lord wanted them to do
in their own communities.

All over the world each year about a thousand young people work, worship, and study together in ecumenical work camps. They combine their work on a project, which serves either the church or society at large, and a demonstration of the fact that the walls of separation have been torn down. Hundreds of ecumenical summer conferences are held each year. They are not merely get-togethers for those who think alike, but are strategy workshops on how to break down the unreal walls of separation between the denominations.

There have been Christian students who went on an "ecclesiastical strike," refusing to be cared for and preached to as long as their denominations separated them. They demanded that their chaplains and churches should recognize that they, all together, formed the body of Christ. There have been youth conferences in which delegates got so impatient with the scandalous division at the communion table that some of them celebrated the Eucharist together, although their churches had forbidden them to do so. They insisted that this act of rebellion did not stem from rash and youthful enthusiasm but from a spiritual challenge to manifest the unity they had received from the Lord.

There are young people who have started ecumenical youth committees and study groups. There are young people who use their holidays to travel to places of renewal in the church of their land and even of other countries. It seems a good time for young people to carry on these activities. Their own churches have said that it is high time for our unbiblical and laming divisions to give way to the manifestation of the unity of Christ's body.

A bit more difficult to handle is the division between the generations. The existence of youth work almost everywhere indicates that it has been and still is necessary to organize the younger generation apart from the adults. In the church, youth work is a questionable enterprise in spite of the fact that it is almost universally accepted. The body of Christ is a symbol of unity; when we refer to the church as the body of Christ, we imply that if one member suffers, all others suffer with him! Can we then divide the church into two or more generations?

In the nineteenth century, the church used the parable of the shepherd seeking out the lost sheep as an example for youth work. That, of course, is nonsense! When we speak about the younger generation in the church, we are speaking about fully incorporated and fully involved members of the same baptized community! Youth work in order to seek what was lost has no biblical ground. No, when youth work is necessary it is because young and old live in different worlds, because they speak different languages, and because they have to face different questions. The gospel seeks people where they are, and youth is often found in different places from the parents. But when the church creates youth work, it should always do so as a temporary solution and hope for the day when we can abolish it.

In the meantime, while we still need separate youth work, we should carefully explore the possibilities of how we can promote the unity between the generations and how we can deepen what unity exists. I know congregations in the United States where one or two members of the session or church council are under the age of twenty. That may be a good idea. Young participants would also do well in larger councils of the churches. Every presbytery, every synod, every area conference, needs to have a few youth delegates with the right to vote and the right to speak. The World Council of Churches has followed this practice since its beginning, and many times the youth delegates have spoken decisively and turned the tide of the debate. The exchange should be reversed: a few of the older members of the church should sit in on the discussion among the younger members of the church.

However, rather than stress youth work, it is much more important that we learn to talk together on real issues. I have found that a discussion on sex is only fruitful when both married and unmarried people are present. If only one of the two groups is there, the discussion is onesided and misses the breadth of the whole church. That is even more true of discussions on social questions and politics. For those conversations we need people who are "in" on the issues and can be party to a real dialogue. To discuss politics with people who cannot vote, or to discuss war without somebody present who was involved in it, renders the conversations sterile and dead.

All this is not said as a plea for the suppression of youth work, but it should be an admonition to keep our youth work small and a service structure for the unity of the whole church.

The most important and difficult of all movements for unity is the one for unity between those people who belong to the church and those who do not. It is most important because we have not been called into the church as an end in itself: we have been chosen for service, and therefore our place is in the world and with its people! It is most difficult because the history of the church seems to point in the other direction. Many fathers of the church have warned us not to be "of one spirit" with the people who have rejected Christ or even not to have contact with them.

Let us look into our relation to the world a bit more closely. We, the Christians, are part of the world. We eat, sleep, and work like other men. We are born and we die, we marry and we have children, we laugh (I hope!) and we grieve like other men. What is more, we have been bound to the others in a special way: we are called to serve them as our master did, who laid aside his divinity, took on the likeness of man, and became a servant. We are called to tell people about our Lord and to live among them in such a way that they will understand what it means to say that God loves the world. We are nothing more or less than the first fruits of the new creation, and we know that Christ is working among those outside the church as much as among us within the church.

We are not "of this world," because we are born of the Spirit, but we are certainly not outside it. Our destiny is not to earn just enough money in the world to be able to keep our real fellowship—which is the church—going. We are called to live a Christian life with others, for others, and visible to others. It seems, therefore, to be dangerous to be always engaged in church work. We cannot very well learn what it means to work in the world and for the world when we are constantly among ourselves, never exposing ourselves to different ways of thinking and acting.

This again points out how dangerous it is to spend too much of our time in church youth groups. It would be much better to have full membership in secular youth organizations and use the church for what it is—a service station, where we tank up and leave. The church is set in the world, not as a separate community, but as a school, in which we can learn something about our job in the world, and as a hospital, where our health can be restored. There we get the vitamins of God's word and the medicine of the sacrament to keep us going on the way.

The way itself is the road Christ took: the way into the world. What we have to show the world is the basic unity of all people who are God's children, whether they like it or not and whether they acknowledge it or not. How we demonstrate this unity is another question. It may call for membership in secular youth organizations. It may call for a careful look at our youth group, which should never become a social community but a study center and a laboratory of Christian living. It certainly should mean that we do not try to make all young people members of our church groups, but make all members of our youth group active members within the context of their own age group outside the church. Such is the call to Christian unity, which is the direct result of the way God lived among us in the person of his Son, Jesus Christ.

So, we have done it. We have not solved many problems in this little book, but we have looked a few question straight in the eye. We have discovered that God is at work in the world. We know that his work results not only in personal salvation for the elect, but that it includes the struggle with the powers as well. We have found our place among men. And our place is not the one of the answer-man who knows everything and has a system into which it fits. Our place is that of the watchdog who barks when the powers get out of hand. We are called to a very exciting and full life. But we shall have to live up to it ourselves!

CHRIST AND THE POWERS

Let us concentrate for one last minute on that strange carpenter of Nazareth, that man who was first hailed by the crowds, later deserted by all, and then became the initiator of a worldwide movement. Let us look at him when he is farthest away from and, strangely enough, nearest us at the same time: Let us look at him while he prays.

As we may expect, he is praying for all men, not only those who believe in him now, but also all those who may come to believe in him later. He prays for us.

"But is is not for these alone that I pray, but for those also who through their words put their faith in me; may they all be one: as thou, Father, art in me, and I in thee, so also may they be in us, that the world may believe that thou didst send me."
(John 17:20, 21, NEB)

What do we think? Can Jesus pray and God refuse to hear him? Or must we now say that this prayer will come true —yes, has come true? What, then, are we waiting for?

Let us join him in his mission, and so discover what the faith is all about and even what life really is. So, up and into the world and look around for the signs of one man—he is there already!

ABOUT THE FORMAT

TYPE: TIMES ROMAN 10 POINT LEADED 3 POINTS
MANUFACTURED BY: SOWERS PRINTING COMPANY, LEBANON, PA.
COVERS BY: AFFILIATED LITHOGRAPHERS, INC., NEW YORK
PAPER: S. D. WARREN'S #66 ANTIQUE
TYPOGRAPHIC DESIGN: MARGERY W. SMITH